GypsyAnge

"The Traveller

A Trip through Time

T.S. DeWalt © 2023

"Book One"

*Taken from real life events and near death experiences
Without being too graphic in nature*

**Copyright © GypsyAngel-Twisted Steel
Publications 2023**

First Edition

Kindle Desktop Publishing

First published in Great Britain

All Rights Reserved

*We are simply creatures of a mindless repetition, caught-up in a wave of
distinct possibility which has been deliberately, slowly, and perhaps even
painfully played out over the course of a great deal of space and time, that
doesn't really exist
But we do what we do regardless, and that's what makes us who we are*

Without limiting the rights under the copyright reserved for this book, no part of this publication is to be re-produced or transmitted, in any shape or form, including photocopying and recording.

No part of this publication may be stored on a retrieval system, altered or transcribed, added to or subtracted from, in any way, shape or form, by any means, without the copyright owner's specific permission.

The named Author (T.S. DeWalt) asserts his moral, legal and God given rights, to be identified as "Sole Creator," of this work, start to finish, including editing, spelling, typesetting, punctuation, language and publishing.

The words within, written or expressed; are merely the author's opinions and/or interpretations of such opinions, unless otherwise stated, and the purpose of this book is to tell a story, or stories, for entertainment only, regardless of those who may, or may not agree with any of its content.

The utmost care has been taken in compiling this book, however no responsibility will be accepted by the publisher, or any compiler, for the truth and accuracy of the information provided, therefore, based upon true events, and providing certain names, times, dates and places, that have been strategically altered, beyond all recognition, this work should only be considered as historical, adult fiction, and any similarities regarding people or persons unknown, living or dead, is purely coincidental, accept for maybe the author himself.

© *T.S. DeWalt* **2023**

For more information on how to order a signed hard copy of this book,
Please email
Gypsyangel@mail.com.

Contents

Book one

Chapter 01: In the Blood.
Chapter 02: The Highway.
Chapter 03: In Memory.
Chapter 04: The Man at the Back.
Chapter 05: Perverts and Pretty Women.
Chapter 06: Home is where?
Chapter 07: Controversy or Control.
Chapter 08: Crowded Trains.
Chapter 09: Heaven or Hell.
Chapter 10: The Emerald City.
Chapter 11: The Edge of the Abyss.
Chapter 12: Dead Man Riding.
Chapter 13: Recollections.
Chapter 14: Twisted Steel.
Chapter 15: Shamaiya.
Chapter 16: The Hotel.
Chapter 17: Another Trip to the Past.

****

Dedications

*To **Sharon**, the love of my life and my very own earth **Angel**, without which, none of this, would have ever come about. You've made me want to be a better man and I've lived my life for that, I've lived for you, I've lived for ours, and I live for what we are together.*

And to all friends and acquaintances, both known and unknown, who have accompanied me on this journey, in one way or another, not least of which, are those of you who are actually reading these words right now.

I thank you all and I wish you the best in everything that you do.

Prologue

There are those who have walked this earth, with a specific purpose, travelling from here to there, searching for a person, or persons, to communicate a certain kind of knowledge or perhaps forbidden information, that may have been lost and forgotten, centuries ago.

They call these people "Travellers" and they appear at various intervals throughout time, conveying messages that either help, or hinder humanity in ways that's never been seen before.

Some say, that there are many that do this, while others say that its only a few, with the power to travel through space and time, perhaps altering their shape, size, colour at will, and showing-up, whenever, or wherever they desire, for whatever reason?

Who the Traveller's are, and where they came from, remains a mystery? What they want and why, is debateable? How many times they've been here before? How many times they'll come again, is also unknown?

This is the story of one mans encounters with them.

1
In the Blood

I've travelled this world for most of my life, lonely days and restless nights, *I've seen a lot of heartache, misery and pain, I've seen a lot of good people, die in vain and then I saw, I saw you, standing there.*

I never thought I wanted much in life, fortune and fame, passes by. *A little bit of money, when I try, a whole lot of loving before I die, and then I saw, I saw you standing there.*

When I saw you standing there, the light was shinning off your hair, *like an Angel I declare, you were standing there, you were standing there.*

And now that I found you, I'll never let you go; *the love that surrounds you is all I know. You are my Angel, you are my light, and I will love you for the rest of my life, since I saw, I saw you, standing there.*

****

He was brought into this world, just before mid-night, with a large amount of blood on the ground, fire in the sky, heavy smoke rising-up through the air, and a lone wolf howling, somewhere, way off in the distance.

There was a dark, shadowy-type of figure, that was probably a large bird of prey, silhouetted across a full moon, which was raised-up high, into the midnight sky, far above the haze, and way beyond the stench of a fading desert, during its pre-dawn, summer's flight.

It was bound to be a troubled life, right from the get-go, as they pulled him out of his dying mother, and laid him down in the cool night air, perched upon a raggedy old bedroll, and wrapped-up in a crusty used blanket, right next to the twisted remains of an old motorcycle that had definitely seen better days before it was ridden down south, along a large empty span of deserted highway, that had taken them all to the wrong side of nowhere, and would ultimately lead him through a life of hell, before he finally hit a dead-end, and no matter how many miles he'd have to travel first, or which way he was forced to go?

He had a head full of dark and mysterious secrets back then, that have haunted him for much longer than he could ever remember, along with past-life memories, and curiously tainted, but quite colourful delusions, that usually came to him from right out of the blue, and then left him just as quick.

There were abnormally intensive nightmares along the way as well, which often consisted of a somewhat distorted, yet unknown future, that never quite seemed to come about as he fully expected, but they certainly did come close at times, he would tell you that.

His father had been a biker, lost to the freedom of the life that he chose, and the course that he plotted on that fateful night. His grandfather had been a cowboy, who owned one of the largest ranches in the State of Texas at the time, and his mother? Well, she was a full-blooded Cherokee Indian, who had once told him, in a vision of course, that she wished that they had dropped him instead of that motorcycle that night, which he never argued with, because he knew that he'd been on one hell of a ride ever since.

****

Now a newborn-child, wouldn't have remembered any of that, but about a year later, my brain engaged, my memories kicked-in, and my world was turned up-side down, yet again. Then I slowly began to realize, that my future was being written out in ways that I had no control over, nor did I have any say in the matter what-so-ever.

I didn't like that, in-fact I still don't, but no matter how hard I've tried to change things, I've had to live with them as well. So I reckon it's time that it was all written down, just to set the record straight.

2
The Highway

"I've never seen anything like this before, have you Bill? Robert said, as the two young Highway Patrolmen walked back to their vehicles. We hardly get any traffic out here, let alone motorcycles, except for ours of course, especially at this time of night or should I say morning? I wonder where they were headed to at such an hour. There's no hospitals around here, in-fact, there's nothing else for at least a fifty miles in all directions. It's just an empty desert, an old military plot if I'm not mistaken, taken from some Indian tribe or another, decades ago, and then left to go to waste as per usual. I don't even the army uses it anymore; I think they stopped using it years ago. Where do you think these guys were going to and what were they doing out here in the first place?"

"I don't know what they were doing out here Rob, his partner Billy said, but if you think that's strange, wait until you hear what the farmer's wife had to say about it all, she figures that if she hadn't pulled that kid out when she did, and wrapped him up like that, he would have died for sure, maybe he still will, we'll just have to wait and see about that, but what else was going on, seems pretty unbelievable, in-fact, you'd probably figure that she's just a plain ole crazy type, because her story is something else."

"What do you mean, Robert said, she's alright ain't she?"

"I don't know about that neither, Billy said, she's pretty weirded out right now if you ask me, shaking like a leaf, hyper as hell, and as pale as a ghost. I know she must be close to seventy by now, and probably has some sort of medical condition that she didn't mention, but there's more about all of this, that just ain't adding-up and I find that a bit unnerving to tell you the truth, really unnerving when you think about it, and I don't believe for a minute, that this was all a simple road accident neither. I mean come on; you just don't lay a bike over for no reason, especially with a pregnant woman on the back. Something caused that, something that we haven't found out about yet?"

"Like what? Robert said again, what did that old woman tell you?"

"Well, Billy said, I don't know what to make of it really; she told me, that she and her husband, were on their way home in their pick-up truck, after shopping in town for most of the day. Apparently, they also went to dinner, and then they saw a movie at the picture house on 9th avenue before they left, so she knows that it was well after ten pm by the time they headed out of town, closer to eleven she thought.

She also said that they were probably only going about sixty miles an hour in their old truck when out of nowhere, a motorcycle flew by them, like the devil himself was chasing it. Her words not mine.

She didn't think much of it at the time, because it went by them so fast that she couldn't tell who or what was on it, and it was clean out of sight in no time at all. But then, about a half-hour later, maybe less, they came upon the crash.

They could tell straight away that two people were dead, or just as good as, that was only too obvious she said, but then she noticed the woman was pregnant, very pregnant she said. So she told her husband to go back into town and get some help, while she stayed with the woman, hoping to birth the child.

She told me, that she had had seven kids of her own through the years, so she knew what had to be done, even if she had to cut the baby out herself, she would, although how she'd do that out here, was a bit of quandary? Again, her words not mine.

By then it was close to midnight, she said, the skies were pitch-black, and a fire was burning somewhere, the smoke was wafting its way across the ground, but there was also a full moon shinning, so she could see quite well, and this is where it all started to get pretty weird for her.

She watched her husband drive away of course, and then she turned her attention to the woman, checking her pulse for any signs of life, and sure enough, there was a weak pulse and some shallow breathing, but the woman was bleeding profusely from a head injury, broken arm, and the skin that had been ripped from her back.

She was definitely unconscious at that point in time, and deservedly so, because all of that pain would have been too much for anyone to bear. So the old woman used her sweater to wrap-up the woman's head wound, put her knees up, spread her legs apart and saw that the kid was ready to appear.

It was that crowning moment she said, apparently that's a thing? I didn't know what she meant, until she explained it to me, but that's what she said? Anyway, the young woman's underwear had probably been torn off as she skidded down the road, or maybe she wasn't wearing any at the time? I guess it doesn't matter now either way.

Then all of a sudden, that old woman got a strange sense of being watched she said, and as she looked around, it appeared to her that there were a dozen or so, shadowy type figures, that she couldn't really make out, standing all around her, closing in, in a tight circle, chanting things underneath their breath, things that she couldn't make out, and waving their arms up in the air, almost like they were praying or something?

Suddenly, she couldn't breathe, she said, and she felt like she was about to pass out, so she yelled-out as loud as she could, "Back the hell-up, will you?"

Then, just like that, the figures disappeared, and she was on her own again, or so she thought? She was a bit surprised at herself at that point in time, because she hadn't sworn like that in years, she said. But then right out of the blue, there was an old man's voice talking to her, in a somewhat familiar manner, she said, and in a tone that she swore she's heard before somewhere, at some point in time?

"You need to get that kid out of there right now, the old man said quite suddenly. It's almost midnight and he'll die if you don't."

She looked-up and saw an old man with a walking stick smiling down at her, a man who was tall, dark and thin she said, with long flowing white hair, different coloured eyes, and a lengthy scar, that was travelling up and down the side of his face.

"Who the hell are you she said, looking around quite quickly and how did you get out here?"

"That doesn't matter much now, does it Kate, he said, just get that kid out of there, he'll be needed one of these days, and there's not a lot time left, so I'd get to it if I were you?"

"What? The woman said, how do you know it's a boy, how do you know my name, who the hell are you and what are you doing out here?"

"Just do your job woman, and don't be asking any more questions, you'll get your answers soon enough, but now is not the time. This child needs to come into this world and he'll need some help, now is the time for you to do just that."

A wolf suddenly howled somewhere out there in the distance, she said, and when she looked up again, she noticed a shadowy type of figure crossing in-front of the moon, almost like a bird of prey, only much larger than that, she said.

She looked around once more and noticed that the old man had gone, like he had disappeared in a puff of smoke.

Freaked out about it all, she nervously started pushing on the upper part of the pregnant woman's stomach. By then the baby was pushing itself out, and she did her part, as best as she could.

Then it was out, on the ground, and just as the old woman was cutting the chord, the younger woman suddenly opened her eyes and screamed out loud, "Don't let them take my baby, please, for God's sake, don't let them take my baby, I'm begging you." Apparently, she gave up the ghost after that, at least that's what the old woman said."

****

"Wow, Robert said, that's a pretty strange story sure enough, but hey, we are out in the middle of the desert, in the middle of the night, and imaginations can run away from people. Maybe that old woman, wants that kid for herself? Maybe she came up with that story about the mother, just so that she could tell the courts at a later date, you know a custody hearing or whatever? I don't know, but stranger things have happened."

"Did you even look at that kid Rob? Billy asked? Did you see that he has a full head of white fucking hair, with different coloured eyes, and a birthmark running down the side of HIS face? How strange is that, because it's only obvious that his mother was Indian, and his father had dark hair as well?

No, something ain't right about any of this, I can feel it in my bones."

Both corpses have brown eyes. I checked. How do you get different coloured eyes from that, one Blue and the other one Green? It doesn't make any sense to me, that's for sure. No sense at all."

"Well the kids off to the hospital now and I'm sure that we'll find out all about who his parents were soon enough. What a way to be brought into this world though? How the fuck do you ever top that one, Robert said, poor little guy, I hope he survives."

"There's one other thing that that old woman said as well, that really gets to me and I think that even you will question this?
That old man, was tall, dark and thin, she said, wearing a long overcoat, a broad rimmed hat, black jeans and square toed boots, with a walking cane, but he didn't actually speak to her, she said. His voice just came into her mind, and it hasn't really left yet.

That old man is still talking to her, she says, but she's having trouble figuring out what he's saying. He called himself the Traveller, and said that he's been here before, but the best part about it all, is that the old man knew it would be you and I out here on this call tonight.

He even told the woman our names before he left. Infact, he had a specific message for you, a message that the woman was supposed to tell you herself, but she's too shaken right now to talk to anyone else. She just wants to go home and forget about this night forever.

"What was it Robert said, what was the message?"
"She said to tell Reaper, her words not mine, that one day this kid is going to save your life, and you won't even remember that it was you, that helped to save his at the time. But it'll happen just the same.

She also said that over time, you'll go back home, get married, and that the kid will become the son that you'll never have. Eventually, he'll be the one that puts you in your own grave, in a good way that is, when it's your time of course.

~ 15 ~

She also said that the kid is a Traveller as well, not will be. She said the old man reckons that he's headed to something that no-one has ever seen before and when he gets there, it'll change the world.

"Wow, Robert said, so that old man sees into the future yeah? That's what you're telling me? Well, that's a pretty good fucking story alright, but I don't believe a word of it. That old woman's full of shit. She's just twisting your arm; or pulling your leg if you like, because no-one has that kind of power as we both know. In-fact, I doubt if we'll ever see them again, after all, the State troopers are here now, and because there's a child involved, the Feds will be on their way as well. We townies won't get a look in sideways, and this mess will be cleaned up by dawn. Besides that, we need to head back to the office now, the shifts almost over with and they won't pay for any extra time, as we both know as well."

"Yeah, well you go right ahead Robert, I'm going to stick around here for awhile and see what I can come up with. If there were others out here, I want to find their tracks. I want to know where they went to, and who they are, because something about this thing, ain't right and it's really bugging me, so I plan to be as thorough as I can, even on my own time, if that's what it takes. I'll see you later though, you have yourself a great day."

****

Reaper didn't think twice, he just jumped on his bike and headed off like a man on a mission. Billy watched as he left and then he watched that old pickup truck head its way down the highway as well. The State troopers didn't stick around for long; to them it was a simple accident with nothing to write home about, so he was left out there on his own pretty damn quick.

Everyone remembered him standing in a field, looking down at something with a flashlight in his hand, but no-one actually saw him leave. No-one was there to see him leave, or were they?

Some folks say that he just jumped on his motorcycle and headed for the coast afterwards, some say it was the mountains. No-one knows for sure? All they really know is that ***Billy Lee Brixton*** was never heard of again, and that he didn't even collect his final pay check at the precinct that had been waiting for him to pick-up that very morning. Oh well, people disappear all the time, some may even want to, while others, simply have no choice in the matter at all.

3

In memory of *Robert T. DeWalt*
Aka, *"Reaper"* (1918-2021)

Already Gone

Life is music for an eternal soul, and the sound is never ending. Cares and woes will come and go, of that, there's no pretending. All we can do, is ride-on, no matter who plays that tune, and one day, before it's gone, get back together, Underneath that silver moon.

****

This'll be my last journey here, he said, but I'm sure, it'll be one that I like. Surrounded by brothers, family and friends, each one of them, up on their bike.

It's a trip that's been done before, we know that one for sure, but it's also the one where my ass won't get sore, because I'm comfortably numb now, there's no pain anymore, and let's face it, they say, that there's no cure.

In a short while, there'll be some sadness to face, but regardless of that, I'll be out of this place. So don't worry about me being left here alone, because I'll be out riding the highways that I've always known?

Sunshine or starlight, I'll be riding through those hills, around long sweeping bends, without any spills, with the wind in my hair and the sun on my face, and no bloody helmet, now that's what you'd call Ace.

There's no heavy traffic, no bicyclists abreast, nothing to meet me when I reach the hills crest. My ride does a ton, runs as smooth as a dream, and there's no fuel needed, I'm like a cat with the cream. And as I ride to the distance, I'll leave you behind; but you'll always be there, in the back of my mind.

My spirits on earth, maybe perched in a tree, but at night time I swear, I'll be the brightest star that you'll ever see.

So smile just a little, when you sense my breath pass by your ear, it won't smell of whiskey now, so there's nothing to fear, and try not to shed too many a tear, but if you find that you must, remember our years and please, don't stay there for long, because we all know that, that would be wrong, and always remember, when the storms come along, take a little time and listen to one of our favourite songs, and know that you can be strong, because you will be, even though I'm already gone.

Robert T. DeWalt, 2021

****

Back in the old days, we would've probably propped-up his open coffin, with him in it of course, somewhere near the corner of the clubhouse walls, leaning it, in a fairly upright and secure position, with a lit cigarette in his mouth, along with an extra-large schooner of wine, whiskey, vodka, or maybe one of his favourite dark beers, duck-taped to his cold, dead, lifeless hand.

He'd have a pretty good pair of sunglasses on, wrapped-up tight over his eyes, with a soft leather skull-cap, or a great looking cotton bandana tied around his head and he'd be wearing one of his favourite long-sleeved, Pendleton-type shirts, black Levi-jeans, a black-leather vest, and some comfortable riders on his feet, all dressed-up to the nines and going out in style, and there'd be a couple of young, voluptuous, long-legged, good-looking, scantily-dressed little honeys, standing by his side, attending to his every need, overseen by a Sergeant of Arms, and couple of pumped-up prospects, that were simply putting in their time.

His colours would be resting on the back of a chair that was sitting close to his feet, with his favourite skid-lid, wallet and gloves, laid out on the top of it all, while one by one, the band of brothers, sisters, relatives, and true friends, would slowly toast to his passing, shot after shot, after shot.

Certain words would be spoken, tributes would be given, and a visible changing of the guard, so to speak, would eventually take place. Votes would've been previously cast, and players would've already been chosen to play. Nothing taken for granted and nothing left to chance.

A couple of hours later, depending on the mood, and whether or not the family was really ready, we'd finally close the lid on the coffin, carry him out to old Willies side-car rig and then carefully strap him into it, before we all headed down the highway, towards an ancient churchyard, with its crowded and overgrown cemetery, where, like so many of our fallen brothers and sisters, that have left here before us, he'd be carefully laid into his final resting place, within a grave that was already dug out and waiting.

It wouldn't be much different to a poker-run on a sunny afternoon really, with the rank and file, specifically lined-up behind us, travelling side by side, on their trusted, American made, V-twin machines, riding at close quarters of course, each one vying for their own position, hoping to help place the coffin into its final resting place, and lord have mercy on anyone that tried to squeeze themselves into the procession that didn't belong, because that would have been a big mistake on their part, huge in-fact. But hey, this ain't the old days anymore, in-fact, it's far from it.

****

We laid Reaper to rest on the 28th day of March, in front of at least a hundred and fifty of his closest friends, family and allies. All of them were brothers and sisters of the road that he had once travelled down, regardless of the motorcycles that they owned, their ability to ride, or whether they had even chosen to ride a bike at all.

The sun was shining, the weather was warm, and the skies were clear, blue and bright. You couldn't have asked for a better day, particularly from an old bikers point of view, and there were moments when it felt as if the man himself, was smiling down on each and every one of us, especially as we listened to the first song of the service, which was not only one of his favourites, but hopefully, what he was finally able to achieve, during the last few moments of his life.

It was of course, Pink Floyds "Comfortably Numb"

His wife, adopted children and close family members, sat in the first rows of the chapel, with the rest of the pews completely filled, along with many more of his friends that were left standing at the back and even out the door.

Not a bad send off for a man that was over a hundred years old, a man that didn't look or act, half that age, a man who was still riding and attending church meetings down at the local clubhouse every Friday night like clockwork, and if it hadn't been for the Cancer, then he'd probably still be doing that. It's what he was; who he was, and he loved every minute of it.

****

The service was conducted by a close, personal friend of his, and it was one of the best services that I've ever attended. It wasn't religious or pretentious in any way, shape or form and yet, it was done with a great deal of respect, along with some true style, straight from the heart, with a lot of careful thought, love and grace.

His casket was adorned with pictures of motorcycles, with all the riders lined-up in a row, standing next to their machines with their headlights on, and pointing outwards, completely wrapped around it, in a circular fashion, hopefully providing him with some memories that he could take on his journey to the hereafter, and then of course, his favourite helmet, gloves and jacket, were lovingly placed on the top of it, also facing outwards, towards the door, ready for that one last ride into eternity.

Tributes were given by many, and tears that were shed by a few, especially when Reaper's own words, were carefully, and quite passionately, read out to us all.

They told us a little about his life, his love and his passion, for all of the things that he had ever done and of the people that he had known through the years.

His only wish was to have had more time, in order to attend his youngest grand-daughter's wedding, but unfortunately, that, just wasn't meant to be.

There was a good deal of sadness that day, just as he had predicted, and hearts were broken, but there was a lot of joy as well, filled with love, warmth and respect, for an astonishingly kind and gentle soul, along with so many magnificent memories of the life that he had once lived, a life that was always lived to the HILT, with a great deal of Honesty, Integrity, Loyalty and Trust.

In his final moments, you could tell that he wanted nothing but the best for us all, and it showed in the service that he himself had planned.

The last song of the ceremony was also another favourite of his and it was played as a loving tribute to his younger wife, whom he had always adored, even at a distance, long before they ever got together. It was of course, Guns and Rose's "Sweet Child oh Mine."

****

Afterwards, we got together at a local bike Café, in a small village on the outskirts of the city, to continue celebrating the life that we had all come to know and love. The life of a biker, as well as a friend, who had also been a father and a husband, a teacher, a warrior, poet, prophet, angel, and at certain times, even a demon of the road that we all travel down, and once again, the place was filled with people, who eventually spent several more hours, happily recollecting on what ***Reaper, AKA, Robert T. DeWalt,*** had meant to them, and I'm quite sure that he wouldn't have wanted it, any other way.

******

4
The Man at the Back

There was something vaguely familiar about the man standing at the back of the funeral home that day. Something, that I'd seen somewhere before, at some point in time, but I couldn't quite put my finger on it for the life of me?

He was odd, tall, thin, dark and mysterious, almost a shadow of figure, who was leaning quite heavily, on a twisted old walking stick, that had a small hand-carved, crystal skull sitting at the top of it, quietly paying his last respects to Robert T. DeWalt.

He had the appearance of an ancient prophet, or perhaps some kind of magical seer, with long flowing white hair, that was straight and down to his waistline, and he wore a long full length beard and moustache, that covered-up most of the lines of age and accumulated scars, that appeared to be sketched, upon his ancient face.

He was dressed in a pair of black denim jeans, with a black-leather waistcoat, and a road worn, black-leather jacket, that had several small patches on the front it, which had been stitched above the pockets and down the sleeves, as well as two rockers above and below a well-known patch on the back, and he was surrounded by others, who were wearing black-leather jackets as well; however their jackets were nowhere near as colourful, nor as impressive, as his was.

You could immediately sense, this man was probably someone that you'd want to meet, someone that could tell you something about the deceased perhaps? How he lived, what he did and where he'd been to in his life, but I also knew that it would be fairly difficult to do that, especially with all of those other men that were standing around him at the time.

So I waited, took a deep breath, steadied my nerves, and then at the end of the service, as the man was about to walk out the door, I managed to get close enough to ask him who he was? "Excuse me sir, do I know you?"

I could feel the pain and sorrow, that was left in his different coloured eyes, and I could see the long, drawn out scars that were written upon his face, as the man looked back at me and said, "It doesn't matter anymore, in-fact, nothing does, but the truth is, I was a friend, as well as a brother of DeWalt, from a time that seems long ago now, in another place, and a different life perhaps, one that most people around here wouldn't want to know about anyway."

He spoke softly, rather slow, and purposefully, with a slight American accent, that seemed to blend in-between the eastern and western parts of the United States at the same time, and along with that, there was a slight hint of a deep, southern draw that seemed to be thrown in for good measure.

I could sense that he was tired, worn-out maybe, and appeared to be a lot older than what I initially thought, but still, I quickly asked him if he would take some time to tell me more.

He apologized, and then told me that he had a plane to catch, that he was only here for the funeral, that time was pretty precious to him.

He said that he didn't have a lot of it left, but he also gave me a card from out of his pocket, which had some strange markings on it, a name and a logo, with a skull and crossbones at the top of it, as well as an email address at the bottom, that I could probably reach him with, and that's when he said to me, "When you're dead, you're dead. Nothing else matters."

After that, he simply turned away, joining a group of others for a few brief seconds, before stepping into a blacked-out limousine, that quickly sped-up and out of the funeral home's parking lot, and then headed down the road like there was no tomorrow left, vanishing in a fading mist, in-fact, the only cloud around at that time.

I didn't get a chance to ask his name, but I knew that I had seen him somewhere before and I wanted to find out more about him, where he'd been, who he'd known and what he had done with his life? I also wanted to know who he was and what he was to my adopted father, *Robert T. DeWalt*.

So I spent the next few months, trying to find out all I could about this guy. I started out, by sending him emails, but they were never answered. I asked friends and family that had gone to the funeral, if they knew who he was, but most of them, couldn't recall that he had been there in the first place and of course, none of them knew his name or anything else about him.

I eventually got in touch with a few of the bikers that I had seen standing around him that day, but they couldn't seem to remember who he was either, so I went on the internet, trying to make sense of the markings on his card and the logo at the top of it, as well as the name "Rebel Inc", but none of that seemed to make any sense either. There were a number of businesses called Rebel Inc, most to do with tattoos, and I was able to get in contact with a few of them, but none of them knew anything about this old man. So, in the end, I finally gave up, figuring that it just wasn't meant to be.

****

About a year later, and completely out of the blue, I finally got an answer back to one of the emails that I'd sent to this gentleman with that twisted walking stick.

I had asked a lot of questions over time, through the emails of course, without getting any answers, so I was more than anxious to meet up with him again, if only to see what he'd have to say?

He told me, that he was due back in England, during the latter part of July and if I wanted to meet-up then, he'd be more than happy to set aside an hour or two, which I quickly accepted. I was literally over the moon with the prospect of course, because I figured that I could finally find out who he was, what he did and most of all, what he had been to *Robert E. DeWalt*?

I could also ask him to answers the questions that I had already asked him, and maybe, if he'd let me, he'd eventually allow me to include his story, in a book that I thought about writing, which by then, I was sure that I wanted to do, although I hadn't written a book before.

So we arranged to meet up at the same bike café that everyone had gone to after the funeral, although he had never been there before, but he still knew where it was, and he was content enough to meet me there anyway.

****

I arrived early, got a coffee, a fried egg sandwich and a bag of plain crisps, and then waited diligently for him to arrive, sitting by the front windows, looking outwards into the parking lot. It wasn't long before a familiar looking, blacked-out limousine, pulled-up and quickly dropped him off.

I watched as he emerged from the back seat, and slowly limped his way towards the front door. I also noticed that it was the same walking stick that he had at the funeral, but this time, he was wearing a full length leather coat, instead of a biker's jacket, with dark pressed trousers, and a lightly coloured T-shirt. It was hot outside, but he didn't seem to mind the heat much, in-fact he seemed rather chilled regardless.

I met him at the door of course, smiled, shook his hand, and then thanked him for his time, as we headed towards the table. I asked him if he wanted something to eat or drink, but he said that he was perfectly fine at the moment, as he had eaten on the flight over, so we slowly sat down across from each other, looking directly into each other's eyes.

He looked pretty much the same, as the day that I met him at the funeral home. Although it seemed as if some of the sadness had finally gone from around him and I imagined that there was a little more life and sparkle in his eyes now, but I wasn't sure about that? It could've been wishful thinking.

He sat there for a moment, looking at me with a slight smile on his face, along with an intensive glow about him, that seemed almost ethereal at times, and then, there was a slight inquisitive look in his eyes, which told me that I should go ahead and start-up the conversation, just as quick as I could.

"Do you mind if I record this, I asked, as I pulled out a small recorder from the top pocket of my jacket? I'd like to keep things as accurate as I possibly can."

He gestured with his hand and said "No, you go right ahead son, ask me whatever questions you want."

"Who are you? I quickly asked, and what were you to Robert?"

"Well, he sighed, that's a pretty long story now, one that started out years ago as you can see, and I'm not sure if I'm ready to tell it to anyone yet. I've never been one to talk about my life in the first place. Where I've been, who I've known, and what I've done in the past, has always been, pretty much, a personal journey for me. I'm a traveller really, one of many, and I suppose that that has suited me fine over the years. In-fact, most people would probably say, that I'm a bit of a mystery for being that way, because I'm as honest as the day is long, although I may appear to be a little shallow with it at times. I don't suffer fools gladly, and never have, but still, they know that I can keep a secret, and if I'm a friend of theirs, then

I'm a friend for life. They can trust in that, and they can trust in me, because my word has always been my bond, and that's something that I believe you should never break.

So, when it comes down to talking about myself, and some of the people that I've known along the way, such as Robert and perhaps, even you now, you can rest assured that I'm constantly guarded with my thoughts, words, actions and deeds, which usually makes things pretty difficult at times, I can tell you that, but still, I'll never say anything that might come back to haunt or hurt the ones that I care about, regardless of what that may be, and if it ends up stretching the truth a little, or maybe even distorts it along the way, then so be it, because my honesty, my integrity, loyalty, and most of all, my trust, will never be compromised, no matter what.

I guess what I'm saying here is this, if I were to tell you some of that, any or even all of it, then you would have to give me your solemn word to be as accurate as you can be, because what you're asking of me, has never been told before, and I'm still not sure if it should be told now."

"I see, I said, and yet here we are, hopefully trying to figure out if any of this will work. Naturally, you have my word on that, but that's about all I can give you at the moment. I don't have a lot in my life right now and to be honest, I've never been one to acquire too much of anything, but I love to write, especially since my latest accident, which you probably know about, right?

I believe that I've been waiting for the right story to come along and when I saw you at the funeral that day, I had a feeling that you'd be the one to give me that, one way or another. I had also hoped that you would feel the same way about it, as I do?"

"Yes, he said, I suppose that I do, but there's so little time left, and we certainly couldn't cover it all, especially sitting here over coffee, which to be quite honest, I usually detest at the best of times, because it doesn't always suit me. I also need to be going soon; because I have some people that I need to meet up with and then another plane to catch of course, but hey, that's what my life is about these days, what can I say?"

"So what do you propose that we do then? I said, because we'll need some time together for any of this to work, maybe a few months even, I don't really know?"

With that, he just looked at me for a moment, and then he put his left hand on top of the skull of his walking stick. He leaned forwards, and reaching out with his right hand across the table, he grabbed my left arm.

There was an immediate, extremely intensive reaction to it, an almost physical type of electrical shock that travelled down and throughout my entire body, from my arms to my toes, and then back up to my head, catching me off-guard and practically freezing me to the seat. I couldn't move, and I suddenly felt sick to my stomach. And then, it felt as if I could hear his voice, reverberating around, inside my head, like the sound of Angel, or maybe a Demon, saying, you will remember.

"You will remember me, he said again, you'll remember my memories, and all of my dreams, and then you'll know what to write, just as if they were your own thoughts and memories, becoming unwound, somewhere in the recesses of your own curious little mind and then, when you don't remember them anymore, I'll return and we'll see each other again, just as we do now, just as we have done before, but of course if all else fails, there's always those damn emails that you like to send."

****

With that, I looked up again, just in time to see him climbing into the back of the limousine, that hadn't been there since he got out of it in the first place.

The driver opened-up the door and I watched as the old man quickly submerged himself into the darkened comfort of that long back seat, without a further glance in my direction. The door was closed; the driver was behind the wheel and the car was speeding-up and out of the parking lot, long before I could even think to wave good-bye.

I was stunned, shocked, and more than a little shaken. Was it something I said? What in the hell have I gotten myself into, I quickly thought? What was this man? Where was he from? And then I realized, after all of that, that I still didn't know who he was? I didn't even know his name.

"Would you like another cup of coffee," the waitress said, just as I was gathering up my wits again.

"I don't think so, I replied, in-fact, I think I've finally gone off coffee, for awhile anyway, and who knows, maybe I'll just stick to tea in the future."

With that I slowly got to my feet and then quite shakily, left the café.

****

I was headed home from that meeting, when I realized that something strange was going on. I couldn't get this guy out of my head, no matter how hard I tried.

It was like his thoughts, words and feelings were implanted, at the back of my own thoughts and feelings, and I couldn't shake it, no matter what? And then I remembered what happened at the café in the first place and how our conversation had abruptly ended. "You will remember, he said, as if my memories were your own."

Wow, what kind of ego is that? I thought. What kind of person would actually say that to anyone? What was this guy? And more to the point, who was he?

I was feeling more uneasy as I pulled into the driveway. I needed to get to the study as quick as I could and then replay the tape that I had recorded during our conversation. There must be something that I've missed, something that would explain more about the way that I was feeling. After all, nobody has that kind of power, nobody.

I opened the door to the study, sat down on the chair, and then opened-up my computer, checking my emails at the same time. Then I pulled the recorder out of my pocket, sat it down in front of me and turned it on, intently listening to our conversation.

What was that? I suddenly thought, as I hit the rewind button and played the same segment over again. "Remember, the voice said, remember."

I played it again, realizing that it had been placed there at a different point in time, because it wasn't part of our conversation that afternoon, but it was there anyway, on the recording, as if it belonged there.

How could that be possible? How could those words be here, if no-one actually said them? How are words, recorded when they're not spoken in the first place?

I listened to the tape again and again, running everything that he said, through my mind, until finally; I was just too tired to think about it anymore. I had gotten to the stage, where I didn't want to remember anything, anyway. In-fact, I wanted to forget about the whole damn thing, feeling like it was a big mistake to begin with, and that my sudden curiosity, along with a slightly morbid fascination, that I must've had for this person, had simply been blown-up, all out of proportion, at a time when I had been caught-up in a minor state of mental fragility.

My adopted father had meant the world to me, for a short period of time, when I was younger, but I had never known where he had actually come from in the first place, or what he had done with his life, before I came in to it.

There were questions that I wanted to ask him before he died, but the timing was never right. I started travelling at a young age, leaving him and his history behind, and now it was too late, leaving all of those questions, unanswered. Anyway, I shut my computer down, got up and went into the living room, turning on the TV and quickly selected a movie which I watched until it was over and then I went to bed. After all, I had work to do the next day and I needed the rest.

It was later that evening, when I was awakened by something eerily familiar, and yet; it was something that I would never have dreamt about, in a million years.

****

"A man walks into a Bar, orders up a drink, and then asks the bartender if his dog bites? The bartender says no, so the man walks over to the dog, reaches down to pet him, and immediately gets bitten. I thought you told me that he doesn't bite, the man said, reeling back from the pain and the simple surprise of it all.

The bartender smiled, handed the man his drink, and then said, "That's not my dog."

****

"It's an old joke I know" the old man said with a smile, while sitting on the big, ole easy-chair that was parked-up in the corner of the bedroom, my bedroom that is.

What the hell? I thought, my wife was still sleeping soundly, but I was wide awake.

I couldn't move though, I was petrified, frozen into place, which wasn't like me, that's for sure.

A multitude of questions were running through my mind, but all I could do was lay there and wonder how this man had got into the room in the first place, where had he come from, and what was he going to do, now that he was here?

"In-fact, the old man just carried on talking, it's actually a scene from one of the movies that they named the "Pink Panther" with Peter Sellers, he said, who plays the rather inept, bumbling, yet fairly comedic, Chief Inspector Cousteau, who's been looking to catch a thief for months on end, but I believe, that it's fairly relevant to the story that you're about to hear, and I'd also imagine, that if you were to think about it long enough, it might even be significant to the kind of life that we all live. After all, who knows what's going to happen to any one of us, at any given moment in time?

We could be walking-up the street and get bit by a dog, or we could have a car accident, get hit by a train, fall down a flight of stairs or endure some other life-ending, body changing event, like you and I have both done, several times in the past, that always came out of nowhere, for no particular reason, yet here we are regardless, trying to pick up the pieces afterwards and carry on with what's left of the rest of our lives, in the best ways that we can.

It's the luck of the draw they say, the nature of the beast. Or is it simply the hand that we've all been dealt? After all, life is just a game at the best of times, and it doesn't seem to matter what happens, when, where, how, or why, because it's all part of the natural order of things, and we know that nature, will eventually run its course, regardless of what we have to say, do, or even think about.

Now, I don't know about you, but I have a feeling, that along with all of that, there are certain unknown forces that drive each and every one of us, down some sort of distinctive pathway, or perhaps, it's multiple paths at the same time, that have been previously chosen, by something or someone else?

A guiding hand perhaps, God, fate, destiny, Angels or demons, real or imagined, that look out for us, as best as they can, steering us all, in the directions that we need to go, whether we want to go there or not? In-fact, I believe that whatever we do in this life, or whatever we've done in the past, has been done before, by someone else, someplace else and perhaps, even numerous times, that are repeated over and over again, throughout the millennia, because nothing in life, has ever been new, or even unique. We're simply creatures of a mindless repetition, caught-up in a wave of distinct possibility, which has been slowly played out, over a great deal of space and time, and we will do what we do with that regardless.

We expect everything of course; but we trust no-one, and then we eventually end up questioning everything, because somehow we feel that life is not what it appears to be, and the only thing that seems to change, apart from ourselves and our positions in it of course, is the language that we speak, along with the words that we choose, and the grammar that we learn how to use, which is often, quite childlike to begin with, but fortunately for most, it usually grows over time, just as we do.

Now, I've always wondered if we could actually control any of that. Or is it beyond our own limited capabilities and complete lack of any comprehension, for the life that we all seem to be living?

Is there a way for us to tap into that repetitious nature, which we all seem to share, and perhaps, alter the course of events, to a much more desirable outcome?

Of course it's bound to be a little different, as to the day and age that we all live in, along with the fact that it's actually happening to us in the first place.

After all, most of us are simply too self-centred, or self-absorbed, to ever look beyond our own lives anyway, so whatever happens; we're bound to take it personal, even though, that has never truly been the case. When it happens though, it makes us all feel completely, and entirely alone.

Suddenly, we find that we're unsure of ourselves and our motives, and of course, extremely confused about why it would ever happen to us to begin with, but if you really think about it, it's bound to have happened before, no matter what it is, somewhere, somehow, and of course, to somebody else, because let's face it, there's been trillions of people, that have come and gone on this planet throughout the ages, and they've all had to deal with their own lives, in the same ways that we have, nothing ever changes.

Take a falling off a horse for instance, or having a motorcycle accident. They are of course, two very different things, and yet both of them are only possible in this day and age. Only one of them, was possible a couple of hundred years ago and perhaps only one will be possible in another hundred years or so. However, the question is as simple now, as it's always been. How many people have done that very same thing, time after time, falling from a horse or falling off a motorcycle?

In reality there are those that have done both. I know that you and I have, too many times to think about really, but I'll get back on them, and I'm sure that you would to.

Now, some people say that when bad things happen, it's simply the sins of the father, being placed upon the son, or perhaps, it's some kind of ancestral curse, that's been handed down through the ages, time after time, that causes such things to happen in the first place, but you might also believe that it's certain unseen forces at work, such as God, karma, fate, the Devil or perhaps even destiny itself.

Still, regardless of the names we give them, and the distinct possibility that there's more than one force involved, they seem to have the power to completely eliminate all forms of coincidence or free-will from time to time, and then replace it, with what seems to be, a pre-conceived outcome, which every one of us, will eventually follow, at some point in our lives, whether we like it or not.

Let's face it; from the cradle to the grave, we make the same journey, regardless of how we go about it, how long it takes, or even why we started out on that journey to begin with?

Contrary to popular belief, very few people will ever question that, and there seems to be little free will in the matter, because each one of us, is led to and guided down a path, which usually makes no sense at all and may never become apparent during the course of our entire lives; however, we will do, what we do regardless and to hell with the consequences.

Each one of us will deal with this journey, in the very best ways that we can, using whatever means and measures that's available to us at the time, never really knowing which way to turn, or indeed, which path to actually follow. In-fact, most of us, are never aware, of any of the real reasons behind the things that we do, as we do them, or even the places that we go to, or the people that we meet along the way and yet there they are, and there we are, just the same.

That may be the most complicated aspect of our own humanity, but in the long run, it will mean very little to anyone else but ourselves, and if we're truly lucky, it might leave a good impression on the ones that we've been closest to in our lives and then of course, the ones we finally leave behind.

If not, perhaps it doesn't matter anyway, after all, with over eight billion people on this planet right now, maybe we're all just a single drop in an ocean, full of love, laughter and light, or perhaps for the many, that may just be emptiness, pain, sorrow, and regret, along with a certain amount of anger and despair.

I know the ones I've preferred, and you can bet that I remember most of the ones that I've been through, but the truth of the matter is, there has been too many times in my life, when I've had to deal with them all.

****

He stopped for a moment, looking directly at me, piercing his eyes into my soul. It was almost like a spiritual awakening, something that I hadn't had in years, but then he just carried on talking like there was something that he really had to say.

Now it seems to me, that there are a lot of people, who are completely unaware of this fact, or perhaps, they simply don't care anyway and never did.

They stumble through their lives, like a leaf, floating on the breeze, or perhaps that proverbial moth, about to fly into the flame. Not much different to the man and the dog, at the beginning of our conversation.

I realise that it's possible and perhaps even probable, that there's nothing more to life than this; however, I personally don't believe that to be true. In-fact, I believe that there is definitely something greater than what any one of us could have ever thought about in the first place. Something far greater than what we have ever imagined or understood, just waiting in the wind, or perhaps, somewhere off in the distance, for all of us to find, or at least a certain few, that care to look for it in the first place. But the problem with all of that is that we live in a world that appears to be, exactly the opposite.

It's a world guided by selfishness, vanity, ego, and an extreme amount of greed. A world, that's controlled by high-finance, government ministers, and corporate executives, who only have money, influence and power, as an interest in life, and to hell with all the rest.

It's a world filled with Capitalism, Commercialism, and Consumerism, where people at the top, always have the most, regardless of what it is that they do, or what they don't do, and they rule everyone else in what appears to be, a never ending game of "He who has the most, wins."

To them, we're only animals, servants, pawns and foot soldiers, at the best of times, to be used, controlled, and manipulated for their benefit only, and then merely left out to die, when it suits them most, while at the same time, they would always have us believe, that we are what we are, because of ourselves, and only ourselves, and that we alone, control that and nobody else.

What we do, and what we eventually become in this life, is simply down to us and there's nothing that could actually change that, because there is no guiding light, no greater power, nothing to see us along our way, and nothing at the end of it all, but pure and simple, emptiness.

We're born alone; we live alone and die alone. We alone, are the sole creators of our own lives and destinies, and it's up to us to figure out whether we succeed or fail, because according to them, whoever they are, there is nothing else and there is no-one else, so all we can do, is make the most of it, while we still can. Of course, none of that may be true at all, because let's face it, it's only a personal observation, taken from my own point of view, over the space and time that I've had, from what appears to have been, a lifetime of ups and downs, ins and outs, good, bad or indifferent, as well as some very sweet and beautiful moments, that have always left me in amazement of the life that I've lived, and yet, here I am, still wondering why I was ever put on this earth, in the first place?

I guess, I'm calling all of that out now, because I've been there and I've done that, and to be perfectly honest, I've always known, that playing their game, has never gotten me anywhere. In-fact, the way I've seen it, playing their game, has only kept us from becoming the people that we should've been all along, and I suppose that that's one of the reasons that I agreed to meet-up with you in the first place; maybe it's time to tell that side of the story and I am hoping that you'll be the one that knows how to write it. But it's really not my story that you should concentrate on, in-fact, it's your own story that people will want read. I'm only here to help you remember it."

****

With that, he just sat there holding onto his cane, as if he was waiting for an answer that I didn't know how to give. In-fact, I didn't even know how he came to be in my room to begin with? I'm pretty sure that I was sleeping when he started-up the conversation and it took me awhile to figure out if I was dreaming or not.

Still, it was a lot of information to process and as I look back on it now, I realise that it still is, and probably always will be, but at the same time, it made perfect sense to me, after all, we are creatures of habit sure enough, and if we don't learn from our mistakes, then we're bound to repeat them, sooner or later.

Is that destined, or pre-destined, I suddenly thought?

Who really knows? I guess the greatest test to this theory, will be the way that you, yourself, react to the words that you've read, and the ones that you're about to read, and then of course, where it is, that we all go to from here?

****

Now the day after that, I had things to do and other meetings to attend, but I ended-up calling in sick instead. I had had a dreadful night's sleep and felt as if I was coming down with something, at least that's the message I conveyed to others at the time, but the truth of the matter was, I had to write down everything that I had dreamt about, before I forgot it, because it had to have been a dream, no matter how lucid it may have appeared to have been at the time. After all, what else could it have been?

That old man had got on a plane earlier that evening, and couldn't possibly have been in our bedroom that night, and not only that; we were alone when I woke up later that morning.

The house was secure; all the doors and windows were locked and bolted. No-one, could have entered the house without me knowing, no matter how much I imagined they did.

So, I went back to the study and sat-down with my computer again. The words were streaming through my mind, and my fingers couldn't type fast enough.

I knew, what I needed to do, and I knew, what I wanted to say, but I wasn't sure where it would lead? And all that time, his voice was still inside my head, telling me more and more as the minutes ticked away. I didn't fight it, in-fact I couldn't and besides that, I didn't want to, so I just let it flow, and for the next few hours or more, I typed out the start to this entire story.

****

5
Perverts and Pretty Women

Let me start this out by saying, I'm old school; I treat everyone as I'd like to be treated. If they're good to me, I'm usually better and I've always been that way.

Respect is a key issue, as Controversial as that seems to be these days. Morality goes a long ways as well, because the older I get, the less I find of that, and I'm pretty sure that that's not a good thing. A man's word should be his bond and his obligation is to stick to it regardless of the outcome.

Too many people don't understand that, and they lie, steal and cheat their way through life, as if there were no consequence to their actions at all. That needs to change, before this world steps into its future. People need to be held accountable for their actions, Leaders need to lead and quit ripping people off. Liars need to be exposed, and the people that wage war, need to have that war, brought to their own doorstep. The world is ready to change; all we have to do is be that change. But that's not what this book is about, although some of it might be?

****

I wasn't born with a silver-spoon in my mouth and I sure didn't have a sliver of gold, silver or a crumpled-up gift certificate, shoved-up my back-side, or hidden away somewhere else, just as dark, damp, and mysterious. But I sure had a lust for the life that I was given and that's just a plain and simple fact.

I was born a fighter, right from the get-go, and I've always reckoned that that's what really counts in the end, because this life is always worth fighting for, no matter what you have to go through to actually live it?

I didn't have a high-paid, smooth-talking, good-looking, slick executive type, as a father figure and I wasn't fortunate enough to have a young, attentive, attractive, affluent socialite, or an extremely elevated professional, or government minister, as a loving mother, and I'm sure I wasn't born royal neither, although it wouldn't have been much of a surprise, if I had found out that that was truly the case.

I wasn't going to be a movie star, or some sort of athlete, or any kind of a high-born society type at all, and I definitely wasn't brought into this world to be a liar, beggar, criminal or thief. I'm just not that kind of person, and I never have been. But I've lived through some pretty wild, crazy, dangerous, and even extraordinary times in my life, and I aim to write about those eventually.

I've travelled to a lot of places in my life, I've known a lot of people, and I've done some incredible of things, but I've always refused to judge, or be judged, by any wealth, property, possessions, or labels, that I may or may not have acquired along the way, because let's face it, it's never been the suit and tie that makes the man in the first place, it's always the way that he wears it, if he wears one at all that is, which I seldom do, and to be honest, none of that's gonna last anyway, because there's always someone around the corner that thinks that they want it more than you do.

Someone who thinks they deserve it more, regardless of the cost, or the sacrifices that you've made, even your own government, or a disgruntled employee, a wife, a husband, kids, or a business partner for that matter? There's always someone waiting to take what you have, not realising, that there's always someone else, who's been waiting to take it from them as well.

Never mind, that's just the way things are. They say it's a dog eat dog world that we live in and eventually everyone gets eaten one way or another. But the truth of the matter is, dogs don't actually eat dogs, they have a lot more sense than that.

****

My life took on a pretty strange set of un-explained circumstances right at the get go, with a lot of twists and turns, that appear to be more than just a little coincidental at times, especially when all the pieces have been put together, and I suppose, that that became the catalysts to writing this book in the first place, as well as living the kind of life, where I was always wondering whether any of it was coincidental, or if coincidence even exists? But hey, I'll let you be the judge of that.

The people who took me in after my birth, couldn't afford, or simply didn't want to keep me in the first place, and like many other kids at the time, I was eventually placed into a children's home, to be adopted out by not so perfect strangers.

It didn't matter that it was over eight thousand miles away from where I was born.

It didn't matter that it was a different country at the time.

It didn't matter that the man who essentially ran the children's home, was the uncle of the man, who adopted me, and it didn't matter at all, that my real relatives, never even signed the paperwork, which really isn't legal in any court of law these days. So I hope you understand why, I might have questioned all of that?

Of course, nothing's ever perfect, as we all know, and I wouldn't want to hold anyone accountable or responsible for any of that today, and to be completely honest, I never really knew what happened back then anyway, because I wasn't quite three-years-old at the time of my first adoption. But I know I went through hell afterwards, and that's something that I'll never forget.

****

Apart from being born premature, with a small hole in my heart, undeveloped lungs, and an inability to move around properly, I also struggled with different kinds of sicknesses, like Polio, tuberculosis, pneumonia and whooping cough, for the first few years of my life as well, which I've always assumed, was actually brought on by the cold, damp, living conditions, that I had to endure back then.

I certainly wasn't alone with that; after all, it was the early nineteen-fifties, and no-one had quite figured out, how to heat-up a house properly yet, apart from a central fire place and a stove in the kitchen of course.

I was frequently ill, in and out of hospital for several months at a time, suffering with bouts of pleurisy, colic and gout, asthma, arrhythmia, mini-migraines that would last two or three days at a time, along with major migraines that would last a week to ten days, or more, allergies, drug reactions and never-ending diarrhoea, along with night-time sweats, bed-wetting, the occasional sleepwalking, and some pretty strange and lucid dreams, that never seemed to leave me alone, as well as a large amount of intense, and crazy nightmares, that I still remember to this day, amongst some of the other things that I truly wished to forget.

I was little more than a year old, when I had my second event, which seared me down to the bone, and literally changed my life forever. Caused by a simple pot of cooking oil that was left unattended, and boiling away on the top of a stove, while an incredibly curious, but slightly frail, baby-boy with blonde hair and different coloured eyes, and nothing on but an old cloth diaper, quickly reached-up for its handle without another thought in his head, pulling it downwards and spilling its contents all over himself.

That was a pretty rude awakening to say the least. A baptism of fire, as some would describe it. Quite possibly the work of the Devil himself, with the mark of the beast left on a throw-away child, that was never going to amount to much of anything anyway, which certainly was the belief of too many people back then, especially afterwards.

Something that would never be forgotten, or forgiven, I can tell you that, etched into the deepest, darkest, memories that I have of this life, along with all of the scars that came right along with it, both inside and out.

That was only the beginning of my journey, and I had already lost my voice, the use of one of my hands, most of my senses, and almost an eye as well, which I certainly wasn't too impressed with, but I soldiered on anyway, as we all do.

I lost whoever it was that was taking care of me after that; No-one ever told me, what happened to her? It's assumed that the bills from my accident were probably too much to handle, but maybe it was something far more sinister?

What I do know, is that I've been told too many lies about it through the years, and I never did find the truth, so I've resigned myself to the fact, that I probably never will. I can only go by what I remember, which, wasn't a lot at that age but I sure did have a lot of visions back then, along with some extremely violent and intensive dreams, or nightmares at times, as I've already said.

****

A broken nose, black-eyes, a cracked-skull, and a pierced eardrum, along with a concussion, at the age of three, through a deliberate act of cruelty and violence, by the hands of a deranged woman, who claimed to be my adopted mother, but had no idea of how to raise a child in the first place, let alone, actually want to raise one, wasn't easy let me tell you.

A year later, it was a completely botched tonsillectomy, at the age of four that had me laid out on an operating table with a sheet over my head, for twenty-six minutes. Just about as dead as dead can be.

That wasn't the first or the last near death experience that I've had in this life, but it was one of the longest. I was out of this world at that particular moment in time, and I didn't want to come back to it, not for love nor money, especially back to such an existence that I'd been living through in the first place. But it wasn't meant to be.

At five years old, my adopted parents got divorced and shortly after that, a friend of mine was raped and murdered, in front of my eyes.

We had taken off to explore the Hollywood hills sign, in California which we did, and then we were snatched-up by some bad people, who took us into a house, and fed us candy. But it wasn't really candy, in-fact it wasn't any kind of sweets at all. It was pills that we were told was candy, and I think that my friend probably ate too many of them at the time.

I don't remember much about it though, I've been told that I've repressed those memories from the back of my mind, but I still remember the cops kicking in the front door a few days later, along with gunshots, and ambulance people taking my friend away. I also remember a man, walking past the police cars, as he came to collect me, and I've had lots of dreams and nightmares about it through the years, but fortunately, they've subsided over time.

Later that year; I got bit by a rabid dog of all things, accidentally of course, but it also meant spending a long, painful week, lying in another hospital bed, having a variety of different tubes and needles, shoved into my stomach on an hourly basis. Naturally, I was sick for months after that.

At the age of six, I was hit by a car that didn't stop, while I was riding a bicycle in the parking lot of a motel that we were staying in.

I can still remember that quite clearly, it was an old black, large, skinny tired, sedan convertible, with two people sitting in the front seat. One was an older man, while the other was a woman, and both of them were in their forties or early fifties. The car itself, was just like what they had in the movies, an old roller type, or maybe a German car with the big front end?

I was lucky that they had used that, because basically, it just ran right over the top of me, after they knocked me off my bicycle first. Of course the cops decided that it was an accident, but cars don't hit kids on bikes, stop, deliberately run them over and then speed away, like nothing had happened in the first place, especially in a parking lot, where they veered into me as soon as they came off the main road to begin with.

I remembered the woman's laughter as well, and I swear I heard her say, "That'll teach him for being a fucking rat." it's a chilling memory to say the least.

We were gone from California after that, and I doubt whether my friend's family got any justice for their loss. No witnesses, no crime they say, pretty sad really.

At the age of seven; it was all of those childhood diseases that got to me, one after the other, like scarlet fever, chicken pox, measles, mumps, meningitis and rubella etc. Of course, I was already jabbed-up to the hilt by then, being a military brat and all of that, but it didn't help.

I suffered from high blood pressure, fevers, migraines, heart-palpitations and jaundice, all at the same time.

There were other moments as well, other incidences or illnesses not worth mentioning, or even remembering, while some of them were simply ones that I've tried hard to forget. Needless to say, there were many times that my young body wanted to quit this world for good, but every time it happened, there was always something that wouldn't let it go.

It's been that way from the start of it all, but sooner or later it'll end. After all, nothing lasts forever and I suppose that when you get right down to it, that's just another reason that I've finally decided to tell this story, so to speak.

Now I know that I'm only one of many in this world, and that everyone has a story to tell. I'm no different to anyone else in that aspect. We all live the lives we live and I'm not making excuses. I'm not looking for any sympathy, forgiveness, understanding, or retribution for that matter.

I'm just laying it out as I lived it. You can make what you will of that.

****

I was picking potatoes out of a farmer's field at seven years old, lugging those hundred-pound burlap sacks to the roadside, as I filled them to the brim, sleeping in an old, abandoned wooden-shack, that had dirt and mud for a floor, and sharing the space, with a variety of bugs, spiders and snakes, along with certain other creatures, that were always lurking around the corner, somewhere in the shadows.

Emptying out buckets of pond scum every time it rained, using whatever dirty old rags, dried-up cow-dung, old newspapers, and semi-fresh straw, if I could find it, to plug-up the holes that were in both, the roof and the walls.

It wasn't easy, and it wasn't sweet, but I didn't have a choice in the matter, it was the life that I was living, and to be perfectly honest with you, it was a whole lot better than what I had already been through, so I didn't complain too much about it. I just did what I was told to do, and that was about all there was to that.

I was given a little dog, for my eighth birthday. It was actually a gift from my first adopted father, who had recently re-joined me, after being absent since the car incident in California, for the last year or so? Who knows where he had gotten to at the time? Probably stationed overseas maybe? But I don't know for sure?

The man had left the military by then and hired on as a farm-hand, spending most of his days mending fences, fixing machines, running errands and whatever else they could throw at him, while I still worked out in the fields.

He spent most of his nights in town, down at a local bike club and a couple of titty bars, chasing women, smoking dope and drinking way too many whiskies, which is probably where, how and why, he got the dog in the first place.

It was a miniature Doberman Pincher that I fell in love with, but as fate would have it, and in less than a month or so later, the landowner's son, who really didn't like me, or maybe he liked me a little too much, turned eighteen, and he was given a 12-guage shot-gun for his birthday.

No-one knows why exactly, but one of the first things that he did with that gun, was to shoot that little dog, right in front of my eyes.

I can't really tell you what happened next, because I was in a state of shock, filled with anger, hatred and rage, splattered in blood, and completely insane with it all by then, but somehow, I ran and got a straight razor from somewhere, and then I ran back to the landowner's son, who was still showing off to the group of boys that he had been with earlier, when he shot my dog.

I quickly walked up to him without a word, and then I tried to cut his throat, but fortunately, the landowners son was a lot taller than what I was at the time, so instead of cutting his throat, I ended-up cutting him all the way down his chest, from his collar-bone, down to his belly-button, giving him a nice, deep gash, that took a hundred-and-eighty stitches to close, and hopefully, the scar that it created, served as a lasting reminder, to never to shoot anyone's dog, nor anything else, for that matter.

I remember the look on his face, as he dropped the gun, and then grabbed his chest. I remember him saying "What have you done now boy?" I also remember picking-up the gun myself, and pulling the trigger at the same time, as I pointed it towards his face, but fortunately, both barrels were emptied by then. I guess we were both lucky for that?

Afterwards, I ran back to the shack with the gun in my hand, not having made any escape plans of course, trying hard to hide myself away in the dirt and the mud, and forget about what I had just done, along with the death of my little dog, that was still laying out in the field, but it wasn't long before they found me there, and after getting my ass beaten by them, and the boys older sister, who had joined them on the search, I spent the next few days, locked in a local jail cell, battered, scraped, and bruised, which I figured I deserved, and then the following months at "Boys Town" for my troubles, which I really didn't deserve at all.

Boys Town was like a boarding school, set-up for convicted juvenile offenders, kind of like the American version, of what a Borstal was here in England.

I was lucky though, I could have been locked away for years for what I'd done, but I convinced the Dr's, that it was a one-off incident, that I wasn't likely to repeat, after all, who could really blame me anyway, it was my dog that the boy had shot, and to me, that was like shooting family, in-fact, that dog was probably my only family at the time, if you really think about it?

My so-called adopted father, disappeared again after that, automatically fired from his job I suppose, and presumably too embarrassed, to stick around anyway, which suited me fine at the time, especially under the circumstances.

Needless to say, my eighth year on this planet, was literally hell in a bucket, and there was nothing that I could do about it, even if it was my fault, as they kept telling me.

****

Now, there were two types of foster parents back then, as far as I knew? Those who wanted sex and those that wanted slaves, and all too often, the two of them would conveniently merge into one, especially during the middle of a long, dark night. It didn't matter if it was a man or a woman, I had already been through both of them by that time and sometimes, it was both at once.

After Boy's Town; I was thrown back into it, but there wasn't much difference being there really, because boys can be cruel at any stage of their lives and they'll always steal, fight, or fuck in a heartbeat, depending on what they think they can get away with.

It's just the nature of the beast, but the fact is, there's too many sick and twisted fuckers, in this world, that don't give a damn about how old you are, who or what you are, or what your situation is, just as long as you can get them off, and I reckon that I was about two years old when I realized that for the first time, no more than three, that's for sure.

Paedophiles, Perverts and Pretty women, I've survived them all sure enough, but that's just another thing that's haunted me for most of my life, along with the people who became such a disappointment to me, because of that in the first place, and trust me, there were too damn many of them.

Relatives, teachers, neighbours and friends, along with correction officers, MP's and psychiatrists, and the list went on. But let me tell you something here and now, there's no excuse for an adult to be fucking around with a child, and it doesn't matter how small your dick is, or how much you twitch, because children, have the right to be children, for just as long as they can be, and the only right you have to that, is to leave them the fuck alone, plain and simple.

This world is sick enough, without putting any of that shit on a child and I don't care who you think you are or what your religion is, it's just wrong, with a capitol **W-R-O-N-G.**

****

I was packing, lugging, and selling fruit and vegetables, along the side of an open road, at the age of nine, and after that I worked in a bakery for a little while.

I helped deliver milk in the mornings and I had a paper route as well, by the time I turned ten. When I reached eleven, I stayed with some bikers in London, and started working on a building site as a carpenter's helper, which became one of my main forms of income through the years, but there was a lot of other jobs that I did along the way as well, and to be perfectly honest with you, there were too many of them at the time, especially back then, but still, I always did what I had to do, no matter what that actually was?

Now apart from time in the Military, being a patch-holder for a motorcycle club and owning my own Roofing Consultancy and General Construction business, I chased storms for a living, I've worked on travelling fairs, spent time as a roadie when I was younger, was a bouncer, a doorman, a body-guard, and a part-time bounty-hunter as well, and yes, I had to shoot a couple of people during that time, in self-defence of course, but that was my life back then, and I had to live it, to the best of my abilities.

I was young, cold, hard, loveless, and probably heartless, during those years as well, toughened by the life that I was forced to live and what I had to do with it, but I took no quarter, and it didn't matter who or what it was, it was always my way or the fucking highway, and if people didn't like that, then they had best be moving on, just as quickly as they could, because I didn't suffer any fools gladly, as the saying goes. I never have and I never would?

I don't regret any of that, it's just the way that I had to live, but I also know that I may have been a little too hard on certain people, other than what I should've been, and I realise that I'll have to live with those decisions, regardless of the way things turned out?

I've collected cars, bikes, dirt-machines, and a variety of scrap-metal for a living. I've worked on farms, ranches, mining fields, and so many building sites through the years that I could never count them all. I've also worked on seismic monitors, and different oil rigs up in the Arctic. Lumber mills and logging camps in the Pacific North West, bars, restaurants, truck-stops, and gas-stations, not only from coast to coast, north to south, east to west, but also around the world at times, and I could never count all the factory jobs that I've had in-between, which almost drove me completely insane, with their incessant little noises, mindless repetitions and never-ending bloody split-shifts.

I hated those times with a passion, and I always will, but along with all of that, I managed to hold positions with prominent and high-profile corporations, like Boeing, the Southland Corporation, Black-Rock and Enron for awhile, which included national-defence contracts, eventually becoming a sub-contractor of choice, to most of them.

There was even a time between all of that, when I was the personal body-guard of a certain VIP, which I may tell about, at some point in the future, just not yet.

Military experience, being a biker, knowing interesting people, certainly got me that gig, but then again, I was probably just in the right place, at the right time.

Anyway, as a Contractor and then later as a Consultant, I was at the top of my field and that eventually took me to the top of some of America's largest and tallest buildings, like the 747 hanger, in Everett Washington, or the Mall of America in Minnesota. One Union Square, and the Vance buildings in Seattle, the Sears Tower in Chicago, the CN Tower in Toronto, and both of the Twin Towers in New York City, just to name a few. In-fact, I may have been one of the last roofers on top of those buildings before 9/11, but that's another story altogether.

I spent a lot of time chasing storms through the States and Canada, as I've said, which provided me with an extremely good living through the years, while at the same time, it simply trashed any real hope of living a so-called normal kind of life that I may have wanted, and I played guitars, wrote songs, and rode motorcycles through-out those times as well, if not every day, then every single day that I could get.

I've worked from daylight to midnight, seven days a week, doing what I had to do to survive. I've worked four hours on and two hours off, twenty-four hours a day, seven days a week, for months at a time, and I took on three fulltime jobs at the same time, at one point in my life, which really did drive me mad, through a lack of food and sleep, if nothing else? And all of that, was simply because I had to, just to keep a roof over my head, put food on the table, pay the bills, and try to get ahead in this life, the best ways that I could, and yet sometimes, especially when I think back on it now, I realize that I'm no further ahead, than what I was when I first started out all those years ago, feeling like a Hamster, left on a treadmill, running its life away. Who would've thought?

****

Now I suppose that people might think, that that was a pretty charmed life, and I'm sure that I wouldn't argue too much about it, because I know just how lucky I was, to have been able to live it. But there were other times, I was homeless, jobless, helpless, and completely hopeless, not ever knowing what the next minute would bring, let alone another day, and you can bet that I prayed to the Angels, to never be put there again, because I had already lost most of my mind, half of my senses, all of my family, most of my friends and sometimes, I had even lost every bit of meaning, and desire that I had for life itself, but I'm still here, and I reckon that I will be for awhile.

And through it all, I've heard the voices of the dead egging me on, and I've seen that proverbial light that shines so bright at times, at the end of a very long, dark tunnel and you can believe it when I say, that there's been more than just once or twice in my life, that I've had to travel up and down its entire length.

I've also been told by some of those that have left this earth before me, that there is definitely more to this life than what we will ever know?

Hell, I've even talked to God, or at least what my idea of God truly is, and I believe that he or she, has answered me back on more than one occasion, and maybe even the Devil himself, has had a few things to whisper in my ear as well, if I only stopped to listen that is?

I was never materialistic, or even interested in a lot of money as far as that goes, although I've owned several different types of businesses, with a few houses and properties etc, but unfortunately, I could never seem to plan for much along the way, because I found out a little too early in life, that plans, like promises, get broken, and then all that you're left with, is an incredible amount of heartache and pain. So, I've tried to avoid situations like that whenever I could, although I realize now that it wasn't a possibility in the first place, because there was always going to be those "ties that bind," that everyone gets attached to, like my little dog "Red" when I was eight-years-old, and it's the same for everyone, no matter who you are, where you come from, or where it is that you think you're going to in the first place?

From the time that I was four years old, lying dead on an operating table, for those long, suffocating, twenty-six minutes, right-up to my latest accident, that stopped my heart from beating for a few brief seconds, something has been here for me, something has been looking out for me, something has been watching over me, something has also been keeping me moving along, and I believe that it's still here.

I'm sure that it exists, but I have no way of proving it. Infact, I don't know what it is, but it's always been here. I can feel it, I can taste it, but it's only when I get close to death, that I actually get to see it, which is a shame really, but in the end I know that's the way it has to be, because let's face it, everyone wants to go to heaven at some point in time, if there is one that is? But nobody wants to die to get there, and who could blame them for that?

Maybe it's true, that only a few of us, will ever get to feel what I've felt, but it's a feeling that I've had for most of my life, and it's also a belief that's never changed, no matter where I've been, or what I've had to go through.

****

So, the question here is this. Does any of this make any sense to you? Because I have no idea about that, so I'll just leave you to be the judge of that for now, and hope that by the time you finish reading this book, you'll get to know some of the things that I already know, but then again, maybe not? But let me assure you that this isn't about what I believe, or what anyone else believes for that matter, it's just what I've lived through. You can take that for what it's worth?

****

6
Home is where?

Right now I live in a house with an incredibly grand, palatial type of view that spans for at least fourteen miles, across an incredibly long and low valley, which slowly drifts into a cool, crisp, shallow and almost lazy kind of sea that most people refer to, as the English Channel.

On a good day, when the sun is up and shining bright, and the weather is cool, crisp and clear, I'll sit outside on a self-made wooden-deck, drinking a glass of lightly spiced, sun-baked, lemon tea, curiously watching, as the ships sail by in the distance, mentally taking notes of their shape, size and speed, while at the same time, silently wondering, where it is, that they might be headed to next.

Of course, there's an app for that these days, telling me exactly what I want to know about them in the first place. Where they've been, where they're going, how big they are and whom it is, that actually owns them all etc. But somehow, that information, just takes away the magic of the moment, so I seldom use it.

There's also an app for the airplanes flying overhead as well, which are usually on their way to or from Gatwick airport, or perhaps its one of the smaller airports in the area, but it's the same story for them, I still prefer to use my imagination, or at least, what's left of it, anyway.

Far from being a palace though, my home is a simple one-bedroom bungalow, sitting on top of a hill, close to the end of a cul-de-sac, right next to what used to be a Bed and Breakfast that some really good friends of mine once owned, and it's slightly elevated above a town called Heathfield, which is comfortably nestled into the hillside of the Wealden district, which is an area of natural beauty, or so they say, deep in the heart of East Sussex, in the southeast corner of England.

The house is a little older than I am, it's a little run down to be honest, a little worn out, a little crooked, broken and bent, but it's a house that's lived in, and it's filled with the love of those, that I simply wouldn't have traded for the world.

People have asked me, "Where you from Mate?" What are you doing here? Why? And I generally tell them that this is my home, and that there is no other place that I'd rather be.

They usually leave a little miffed, slightly curious, and totally confused, because I don't sound like I'm from here at all. I certainly don't look like I would be, and I guess that I don't act like I am neither, at least some of the time. But to me, home has always been where the heart is, and this place along with its people, certainly have taken mine.

It's been that way for decades now, and I've loved every minute of it, but before that, I spent most of my time travelling, continuously searching for something that I never found. Wasting so much of my life on trivial pursuits that were never too close to my heart to begin with, and endlessly chasing that power, fame and fortune thing, along with the broken dreams, that I may have held back then, like the ones that most of us find, never come true anyway, no matter how hard we try.

I've come pretty close though; I'll have to admit that. Infact, I've succeeded in more things, than most people will ever get to try and do in the first place, and I know that I've had my share of some really good times doing it, but I also know, that I've had a lot of bad times as well.

I've climbed some of the highest mountains, in some of the strangest places and I've seen what life was like on the other side, but I've also been to the bottom of some of the lowest valleys and pits, that you could ever imagine and trust me, I didn't like what I saw there. Not one bit.

I'm guessing that that part of my life is almost over now, but you never really know what's around the corner these days. After all, things have a habit of going bump in the middle of the night, and then the what was, or the what is, suddenly becomes, the what could've, would've, should've been, and there's very little that anyone can do about that. Besides, I'm nowhere near as young as I used to be, nowhere near as strong, healthy, or as restless as I once was, and I suppose that in the grand scheme of things, there aren't many dreams left for me to even try to make come true anymore, at least, for myself anyway?

But I guess that's alright, because I've done my time. I've played the game, and I know deep down inside, that I played it, about as well as anyone could.

I didn't win anything of course, but then again, maybe no-one ever does, because that's really not the point to begin with, but I gave it my best shot, and we all know that you can't ask for much more than that now, can ya?

So I sit here, trying to remember the stories of my youth, along with different parts of the life and times that I've lived, for as long as I'm able to and hopefully, I'll be able to invest whatever time, effort and income that I might have left, into this house and it's amazing surroundings, for future generations that will want to feel the love, comfort, compassion and warmth, that this building, house and home, has brought and then of course, I will also keep on supporting my wife, family and whatever friends I may have left, as well as the local community, in whatever ways that I possibly can, and who knows, maybe one day, I'll be able make someone else's dreams come true, or at least, help them along their way?

****

Oh sure, I'll still travel, but it probably won't be around the world anymore, because there's really no need for that now. I've been there and done that, and to tell you the truth, apart from private, corporate or even military travel, I've had a gut-full of all those high-occupancy, low-altitude, so-called commercial flights, with their nervous, sedated, or completely inebriated, self-centred passengers, that usually end up, very loudly, regurgitating in their seats, and then throwing-up their liquid breakfast, lunch or dinner, into an already used, plastic lined, paper sack, which they inevitably try to hide, somewhere deep in the pocket, that's located on the back of the chair, that sits directly in front of them, usually, without a single thought or a care in the world, for whom it would be, that actually has to fish it out, at the end of the flight.

While at the same time, their darling little angels, are creating havoc by running up and down the aisles, yelling and screaming at the top of their lungs, dodging all of the passengers that would surely like to wring their pretty little necks, if they could only get away with it that is, until finally and usually quite abruptly, they too, suddenly start to shake, spasm and vomit, which quite unnecessarily, ends up spraying everyone else around them at the same time.

And I certainly won't miss any of those tired, worn-out, over-worked, under-sexed, slightly ill-tempered, hosts and hostesses, that simply can't be bothered to do their jobs right on a good day, let alone in the middle of the night, because of jet-lag and a 24 hour party that they attended, right before they boarded the flight in the first place.

Nor will I miss those funky headphones, micro-shots, magazines, and fantasy travel books, along with other personal, supposedly low-cost, duty-free items, that usually get themselves, strewn about, here, there and everywhere, that they shouldn't be, because of high turbulence, bad weather, and a piss poor choice of route to begin with, causing the half-drunk, half-stoned, or completely half-witted pilots, along with their crew, to carefully manoeuvre their way around them, much like an obstacle course, as they slowly lumber by, forwards and backwards down the aisle.

Then there's those incredibly long and boring queues, with mile after mile, of carry-on luggage, accompanied by what seems to be, so many more wasted hours, filled with the noise of a big-top circus, complete with clowns and all their animals, waiting for their passport stamps, along with a slew of extra questions, that you know, you have already answered on all those bloody forms, that you really couldn't see to read in the first place, and last but not least, there's all those cranky, high-nosed, inquisitive, stuck-up, so-called customs officials, that truly believe that they have every god given right to detain and harass you, simply because you might look or act a little different than the rest of the people that live in the country that you're visiting to begin with. And all of that was on a pre-booked flight that you inevitably paid way too much for in the first place, hoping to avoid the exact same situations that I've just described. But it sure beats the hell out of sailing, where you still have the lengthy queues, the kids, the clowns and the baggage, and of course, the wasted boarding time, just so you can spend the first week clinging to your bed, because you can't find your sea legs and your head won't stop spinning. The second week, simply bores you out of your ever loving mind, with old movies, bad food, too many stupid people, not enough space, and a lack of good entertainment and then the third week, is usually spent, with most of your time, simply wondering why in the hell you hadn't taken that bloody airplane flight to begin with?

Besides that, with the way that computers are these days, I can easily trip around the world and see what I want to see, without ever having to leave the comfort of my own home. Who would've thought?

****

Now, don't get me wrong here, because I really do love to fly. It's just that I prefer the comfort of a private jet, or a personal plane, or even a helicopter, for some of those short in-land excursions that we all have to take from time to time, and of course, I've flown down many a highway, sitting on top of my favourite V-twin engine or perhaps even a few Japanese four or six cylinders, from time to time, with two bits of rubber barely touching the ground, and the wind screaming past my ears, as I've cranked up the throttle just as far as it would turn and to be honest, I'd really like to think that one of these days, I'd be able to do all of that again before I shuffle off this mortal coil, but to tell you the truth, that's highly unlikely, because it looks as if those days are over as well, but the memories still live on, for now that is.

****

The SST (Concorde) was a great plane to fly on, over the ocean of course, not quite as good as a Blackbird SR71, but that's another kind of plane altogether.

London to New York, in just under four hours, and then back to Paris in less than five, having breakfast, just north of Tiffany's on fifty seventh and fifth, and a fine steak dinner, somewhere south of the Champs-Elysees.

Yeah, that was the life alright, but until they bring back Super Sonic Transport, or perhaps something even better, then I reckon I'll just stay on the ground and eat my food in the comfort of my own home and it's truly beautiful, but slightly less than majestic surroundings.

After all, I have a lifetime full of memories, that need to be written down, which is going to take years to complete, if I can complete them at all that is, especially as slow as I write these days. Some of those times, were pretty damn good, but a lot of them weren't, and some of them were simply out of this world, but at the end of the day, they are what they are, and they are, all mine.

I can only hope, that you'll enjoy the ones that I share with you and that you'll want to read more of them, as they're written out, because to be perfectly honest with you, that's what this is all about anyway, after all, what good are memories, if you're the only one that can actually use them?

So, where to start? That's always the question, isn't it, no matter what the answer is, and I suppose, that it really doesn't matter in the long run, because the stories are already here; I just have to bring them all out of their hiding places and then put them down on paper for you to read. But, it's never been that easy for me, because I've lived my life, as a pretty private individual, most of the time anyway, and I guess that that has suited me over the years, however, when you're writing a book about the people that you've known, along with the things that you've done in your life, then all of it changes in a heartbeat, and what was once, always private, suddenly becomes very public indeed.

****

7
Controversy or Control

Back in the days when men were men and women really didn't wannabee. You know what I'm saying, maybe a hundred and twenty years ago now, maybe more, long before that Rockefeller Science took hold, with some of its strange, deluded, and completely deranged geniuses, who started messing around with the human genome, trying to turn the rest of us into a new version of "Long Pig" two-point-fucking-zero and then some. Most men and women that lived back then, did whatever they wanted to do, or whatever they had to do to survive in this world and just as long as it didn't hurt anyone else, no-one really questioned it.

They didn't have to ask for permission from anyone, and they definitely didn't need a fancy piece of over-priced, but beautifully framed paper, bought through years of mindless indoctrinations, along with countless hours of sleep-deprivation, and a slave-labour mentality, slowly extracted by a so-called higher educational institution, just to let everyone know that they could do whatever they wanted to do, whenever they wanted to do it. Instead, they just went out and did it, and it was pretty much as simple as that.

If they screwed-up whatever they were doing at the time, then they'd fix it, or they'd find/hire someone else that could fix it and then move on to something else, doing whatever that was, in the best ways that they could.

In the end, they'd perfect whatever it was that they were doing, and they'd be damn good at it. Proud of their accomplishments even, and perhaps in time, they'd become the best of best, real experts of their trade so to speak, and then maybe, they would eventually hand that knowledge down to the next generation, if the next generation could even be bothered that is?

That's how Businesses were built back then. That's how Kingdoms were ruled, that's how the world was run, and that was the way that it had always been, since the beginning of it all. **Just do it.**

****

Of course, there's always been a higher educational system as well, with certain standards that people had to follow, along with rules and regulations, etc. but not for the masses. That was usually left to the upper echelons of a wealthier society, like the religious, or the black arts, or the mathematicians and the astrologers etc.

Common people, poorer masses, were usually kept from such knowledge in the first place and seldom rose above it.

It's not much different today, but there are those who have succeeded in rising above it regardless, and some of them have surpassed what's considered standard practise, changing the boundaries of a system that's been set in its ways for far too long now.

****

I've known that in my lifetime, perfecting so many careers, that it might make some people's heads spin. Learning most of those skills, from the very best of the best, but nowadays, most people will never get to know that kind of life at all, no matter how much they strive and struggle, because it's all been tragically altered, changed with the onslaught of personal Computers and Artificial Intelligence.

****

Let's face it; you can't take a piss these days, without someone knowing about it. They monitor your water, your electricity, your gas, the foods that you eat, the drinks that you drink, the clothes you wear, the places that you visit, even the blood, sugar, and alcohol levels, that run through every one of your veins, and it's all done with computers.

They control everything, from the World Wide Web, to the satellites up in the sky. From the family automobile, to every boat, dingy and ship, that's out on the ocean. They control the planes, the trains, the busses, coaches, and every tank, weapon and bullet, that's utilized in the fields of war. Hell, they even control the soldiers that occupy those fields, and they always have.

They control communication, phones, radio, television, movies and advertising. They control the schools that your kids are in, the hospitals that are needed for the sick and the injured, and the graveyards that are filled with the quick and the dead.

There's nothing that isn't computerised, and whether you know it or not, your own name is somewhere on their list, tucked inside a machine, that's connected to millions of other machines that they control as well. But they can't control your mind, not yet anyway. Not unless you want them to?

****

Don't get me wrong though, because they really are trying to do that. Without your knowledge of course, or your consent, and there's no doubt about it. They've been at it for decade's now, maybe even centuries, and for some people, they've already succeeded. For the others, well, I guess that they'll just die out eventually, becoming some kind of faded memory, lost in a sea of faded memories, oblivious to the grand delusion of things that are still yet to come, and I suppose that someone, somewhere, will consider that to be a win-win situation. In-fact, you could probably bet your bottom dollar on it.

Simply put, they want control over every aspect of your life, and their ability to achieve such a thing, is rapidly approaching the 100% mark, whether you know it or not, or whether you want it or not, and it appears, that no-one can stop it, or so they say, whoever "They" are, that is?

They've taken what was once a living world, and turned it into a dying planet, and the worst part about all of that, is the fact that it's bound to be some sort of computerised, artificial-intelligence, or one of its machines, that out-lasts us all.

****

Call me crazy, but I for one, don't think that that's such a great idea, but at the same time, I've also wondered, whether it's happened before?

Could it be that where we are today, is not really a matter of what "They" call evolution at all, but more like a straight-up, machine made manipulation?

It doesn't make any sense that humans supposedly walked out of Africa Seven-hundred-thousand years ago, or more, and then all of a sudden, within the last twelve-thousand-years or so, they became domesticated?

How and why that happened, should be the subject of everyone's conversation at least once or twice in their lives.

After all, they want you to believe that for **700,000** years, mankind was nothing more than a mass of small nomadic tribes, scattered around the earth, living in trees, caves or Tepees, hunting and gathering what they needed to survive, but somehow, during the last **12,000** years, after a lengthy Ice-age, and numerous world-wide, cataclysmic events, that saw fire, rain down from the heavens, earthquakes, floods, and frequent volcanic eruptions, that surrounded the earth and almost destroyed the atmosphere, they suddenly became aware of a different lifestyle and decided to plant crops, corral their wild animals, and then build roads on difficult terrains, that even animals wouldn't want to travel, along with erecting large stone buildings and brick-houses en-mass, laid out in huge cities to live in. Yeah right?

What really happened during those first 700,000 years, and before that time? Where did we come from, why are we here, and how many times have we been here before, sitting on the eve of destruction, letting these fools rule over us all, and letting these machines rule over them?

Is it eternal? Or do these machines eventually break-down and die themselves? Are we living inside of one? Are we one of them ourselves? Are we living at all?

****

As you can probably tell, I don't believe a word of it, there's too many questions that remain un-answered, and too many other things that remain hidden from us all. Too many things that don't add up, and for someone who loves his math, two plus two, always equals four, not three or five, as some people are trying to make us believe today.

Darwin wrote a book in the eighteen hundreds called the "Theory of Evolution." With "Theory" being the operative word here.

He was paid a lot of money, by some very powerful and influential people that were out to crush religion at the time, which to be honest, had a stranglehold on our society for too damn long. It worked out well and his book became extremely successful, as we all know. Of course those powerful people made sure of that.

Now-a-days, people will try to convince you that his "THEORY" actually meant FACT, when we all know, especially in that particular case, that there are no facts. The math simply doesn't add up.

There are no long term studies, no empirical evidence, and no way to replicate or recreate anything of the sort in any scientific environment, and there's certainly no way to monitor thousands upon thousands of years that have already past. Unless they have a time machine of course, but they certainly haven't told us about that yet.

Now you can speculate about it, if you want? You can debate about it until the cows come home. You can theorize it, and you can believe what your so-called educational institutions have programmed you to believe, for their acceptance of course, but the fact is, for the last **12,000** years at least, man hasn't evolved at all. In-fact we're just the same as we ever were, maybe even less.

Oh sure, we have the technology of sorts, we've got machines and computers, along with the ability to live like Gods and Kings, but we haven't evolved into anything, in-fact, it's pretty much the opposite.

We can't even replicate what the people of the past built during their time, like the Pyramids or mega structures that used hundred ton blocks of stone that were hoisted up four, five, six stories in the air, or more.

Structures like the Sphinx or Stonehenge, or some of the temples around the world that have been carved out of pure granite, perhaps on top of some of the highest mountains in their area, like Machu-Picu, thousands of years ago?

How about the fact, that there was electricity before Edison and Tesla? Flying machines before the Wright bros, electric cars back in the eighteen hundreds, and electronic robots before that? But hey, don't just take my word for any of this, look it up for yourself. I ain't lying to you.

Einstein explained it all when he wrote the laws of Thermal-Dynamics which basically states, that everything, will fall into chaos eventually? No ifs, ands or buts about it.

Yeah, I know he was paid to do that as well, but let's face it, Order out of chaos, simply doesn't happen without a driving force behind it, and every living thing on the planet eventually falls into chaos. It's born, nurtured, grows, gets sustained by others, sustains itself, and then it grows older, gets sick, withers away, and finally dies.

Complexed order, maybe the most complicated in the universe, eventually turns into complete chaos, that's the natural selection of things. That's the survival of the fittest, that's the way it's always been, and that theory has been proven, time and time again.

You can produce it, manipulate it, speed it up, or even slow it down, but you can never stop it, and why would you? It's been that way since the universe began, however many billions of years ago that actually was?

It's the opposite of evolution, something that I like to call Devolution, although that word has been used to mean something entirely different, which makes me wonder why? But it's a proven fact regardless. Replicated time after time, year after year, century after century, and you don't have to be a shill, or have a piece of programmed paper to know the difference, you just have to open-up your eyes.

****

But that's not what this book is about. That's just an opinion of mine, to show you where I'm coming from so to speak, and it doesn't matter whether you agree with it or not, or whether you can even see the same side of things? I'm not trying to argue with anyone here, and I'm not trying prove or disprove anything, I'm just telling a story the way I see it, and as a writer, that's about all that I can do.

My opinions don't matter, any more than anyone else's; I've just written them down for the world to read and I'll stand by them regardless.

I have another opinion before we start the first part of this book, one that I've decided to add to all of this as well, just to let you know where I'm at, as a writer and what I believe may or may not be happening on the world's stage today. But again, it's just an opinion, right or wrong, it doesn't really matter. You can agree with it, or disagree; it won't affect what's already been written.

It's a brief synopsis of the life I've lived, up until a few years ago, and once you've read this book through, then maybe, you'll know why I think the way I do. But let me just say this, I ain't special in any way, shape or form, and I've never claimed to be, because I know that there's millions of others that have had to live their lives just as I have, and millions more that are going to, in one way or another. That's simply the nature of the beast that we all deal with, and there's no getting around it.

****

8
Crowded Trains

Crowded trains, over-booked planes, football, basketball, and baseball stadiums, over-packed and over-stacked, with the mindless, arrogant, often inebriated, self-centred masses that are only out for themselves, regardless of the reason, the season, or even the weather? And the amount of garbage, misery and completely pointless debris that's left behind is overwhelming.

Indoor hockey rinks, outdoor music festivals, packed-up pubs, and stacked-up clubs, that are continuously filled with intoxicated little fools that can barely spit out a complete sentence, or even stand-up straight for most of the time, including yours truly, when I was too damn young to know any better, or just too ignorant to even care.

Private parties and movie theatres, mass demonstrations, and some pretty irate, even intense rush-hour traffic, while standing-still in the middle of the gruelling heat, on a long summers day, somewhere outside of Mobile Alabama or Memphis Tennessee, Tulsa Oklahoma, Dallas, El Paso, Huston, or even Phoenix Arizona, sitting on a large V-twin motorcycle, with no particular place to go, and no real need, or even a good reason, to be there in the first place.

Sturgis and Miami spring breaks, New Orleans Mardi-Gra, Cinco de Mayo and the day of the dead (Dia De Los Muertos) somewhere south of the border?

New-York in the middle of its longest winter, watching the ball drop in Central park, with about a million other people at the time, who were all wrapped-up in their fancy Parkas and blankets, huddled together in three feet of snow, waiting for the frostbite to kick in to their toes, coughing and spluttering from the cold, and then it was on to California, for an even longer summer, while running reckless through the streets with the Watts riots going on, or the ones that were brought on by the injustices of the Rodney King scandal, a decade or two later.

"Why can't we all just get along?" He said at the time, still battered, bloodied and bruised, from police brutality that he had recently received. It was a great question back then, and it's an even better question now.

L.A. to Vegas, Laughlin to Reno, Portland, Seattle, Vancouver, Boston, Chicago, London, Paris, Rome and Madrid. Hong Kong in the middle of the night for an unexpected layover, and Kobe Japan, after the earthquake in "94".

Sitting in a Café in Amsterdam, Luxemburg or Istanbul, Military service in Viet-Nam, Laos, Cambodia, Germany and then down in South America afterwards.

Alaska to Bimini, Vancouver to Newfoundland. Greenland, Iceland, Australia, New Zealand, the South Pacific and of course, a beautiful little Island that I call home, that's stuck out in the middle of the North Atlantic.

****

Altogether, I've travelled to a lot of different countries, including every State and Province, both north and south of the US borders.

That's a few billion people that I've shared airspace with, at one time or another, and all of that, was during some kind of epidemic, or so-called pandemic. But I've never seen the amount of lies and so-called misinformation, or the likes of what's been happening today, and I truly hoped that I never would?

****

I've never seen the western world, completely shut down, with everyone who wasn't in government, forced to wear a mask, stand six feet apart, ignore the sick, the elderly and the dying, and then be coerced or even forced into taking a new kind of mandated, genetically modified, Synthetic Injection, regardless of whether they wanted it or not?

I've never seen so many people, who have basically given-up on their hopes and dreams, and their life's ambitions, just to join the ranks of the unemployed, simply because they were told to do so, by some crazy little fascist fool that thinks that he or she, actually has that kind of power and authority over them to begin with.

I've never seen so many farmers forced to give up their lands, kill off their stock, and plough over their fields, simply because of a bureaucracy that should never have come about in the first place, a bureaucracy that should have been stopped dead in its tracks years ago.

I've never seen so many small business owners and shop-keepers, forced to give up their livelihoods and then lock-up their doors forever, and I've never seen so many homeless people, living on the streets of Seattle, Portland, New York and L.A. not to mention every other so-called

Woke-liberal-democrat-WEF-UN-NWO city in the western hemisphere. Like London, Paris, Amsterdam and Rome etc.

It wasn't a virus that did that; it was a New World agenda. The Great Reset, or Agenda 21/30, and if you haven't heard of it by now, then you better wake the hell up, because it's coming to you whether you know about it or not. It's already here and it was planned decades ago.

****

Now, I've climbed to the top of a lot of mountains in my life, and I've been at the bottom of some of the longest, deepest and darkest valleys, that you could ever imagine.

I've travelled through jungles and sailed a few seas. I've stayed in five-star hotels, eating caviar for breakfast and drinking their over-priced champagne for lunch but I've also been homeless, helpless, and pretty hopeless at times, while sleeping underneath the stars, with nothing to eat, nowhere to go, and not a lot to live for.

I grew-up on the streets and learned about life from an early age. I was thrown into it right from the get-go, and I've had to live with that ever since. It wasn't easy and it was never fucking sweet, but all in all, it was still my life just the same and I was content with living it, up until now anyway.

I've owned property, cars, RV's, motorcycles and trucks. I've owned businesses, had partners, and several different careers at the same time, and I've been to the top of some of the tallest buildings in the world, as well as at the bottom of some of the largest.

I've owned just about everything that I've ever wanted to own, at one time or another, but I've also owned nothing at all, and not once did I listen to anyone that told me that I couldn't do what I wanted to do, when I wanted to do it.

Not once, did I let someone tell me that I couldn't have what I wanted to have, when I wanted to have it, and not once did I let someone tell me, that I couldn't go to where I wanted to go, when I wanted to go there.

Now, don't get me wrong here, because I know that there's been too many times that my hopes and dreams have been shattered along the way, and I've always been lied to, by those that think they're better than me, and told that I only have myself to blame for that? But that just ain't the truth, because they've written the rules, that we can only learn as we go along, and if we break those rules, then we're thrown right back down to the bottom of that abyss again, time after time.

And sure, there's been millions of things that I haven't been able to do, when I've wanted to do them, just like everyone else in this world, but that's the life we all live and no-one ever said it was gonna be easy.

However, the one thing you never do is give-up. You don't give up on any of it. ***Not now, not ever, no way.***

****

You don't listen to people that will tell you, that you can't do something, when you know damn well that you can, and you probably already have. You don't listen to people that tell you lies, then break their promises in less than a heartbeat and you certainly don't listen to anyone that doesn't care about you to begin with, which to be honest, is going to about ninety-nine percent of the time, and ninety-nine percent of the people you know anyway, and it doesn't matter who you are, who you think you are, or who you wannabe in the long run?

I started out with nothing in this life, as we all do, and in the end, I'll have nothing to show for it when they burn my body to a crisp or bury it in the ground.

They'll make sure of that. But I'll leave these words behind regardless, how long they'll last, is anyone's guess?

We'll all get there in the end, that's the inevitable part of this life, so why in the hell should we be worried about any of it now, just because someone else tells us to do so?

I don't think so. This is my life and I'm gonna live it the best ways that I can. If anyone disagrees with that, they can go fuck themselves. They don't pay my bills, they don't put any money in my pockets, and they certainly don't care if I'm able to put food on the table, or even keep a roof over my head, and I know that I'm not alone with that. They want everyone like me to simply drop dead, and they want everyone else that's less than fifty, to become slaves to their new world horror system.

I have a problem with all of that, and I'll probably be writing more about it when I can. I just hope that people like you, stick around and read it, and whether you learn anything from it or not, will be up to you, not them, whoever they are?

****

9
Heaven or Hell

Somewhere out there in the darkness, *far beyond those neon lights. Riding hard out in the country and no-one else was in my sights. Just another lonely Angel, didn't have no place to be. Always running from the Devil, and he was slowly catching me.*

Now I came across a woman, *who was out there on her own? Her eyes were blue and bright as fire, but her heart was made of stone. She was standing at a cross-road, in the middle of the night. I slowed down and she jumped on, and asked if I could ride?*

So I cranked up that ole throttle, *past a hundred miles an hour. She could hear that motor purring and she could really feel its power. The moon was up there high above us, as the sky was turning black. We were headed down that road to hell, and we were never coming back.*

Now, I really don't remember, *just how long we rode like that. It might have been a million miles, with her sat there on the back, but somewhere after my sweet Texas, before that lonesome Georgia tide. I swear I heard her saying; you just took this devil, for a long, long ride.*

And now you might just see me riding, *out there every now and then, an Angel running with his Demons, riding high upon the wind. I never know just where I'm going, but I sure know where I've been. You see, I rode that road, right straight to Heaven, down to Hell, and back again.*

****

There was a time when I lived like some kind of jacked-up, modern-day cowboy, out riding the range, on a slick little, dark-painted, one-trick pony, that was always filled to the brim with that liquid magic, surrounded by high polished chrome, soft rubber tires, decorated Italian leather, and a rather large V-twin motor, sitting way down low, humming between my legs, while resting on a hard and rigid, American made steel frame. Back in the days when America still made steel that is.

I fell in love with motorcycles before I could ever ride, and once I learned that, I expected to keep them up-right, straight, and in-between the lines, as I effectively and quite efficiently, manoeuvred them in and around all of the traffic, that was out there with me, somewhere, no matter where that somewhere was at the time?

I had learned to avoid every seen, and sometimes un-seen obstacle that flew my way, for literally decades by then, which always appeared to be waiting for me, like some sort of insanely demented demon from hell, or perhaps it was simply a stone-cold, murderous assassin, who was looking for the right opportunity, and the exact moment to strike. In-fact, there were years on-end, when I'd practically fly through all of those tight, little corners, long drawn-out curves, and sudden lane changes, that were consistently being thrown-up along the way, catching the wind for days at a time, riding at eighty-five plus miles an hour, just about every chance that I could get and always trying to find that succulent little sweet-spot, on my American-made V-Twin motor, while at the same time, enjoying the vibrations that came right along with it, that usually put me somewhere in the middle of a "Mental Zone" that I could never truly explain, or even start to understand? And if I was lucky, which to be honest, I usually was, it was with the wind and the rain, falling somewhere else, way off in the distance perhaps, with the sun beating down upon my back, or the moon, high above, softly illuminating, my way back home, no matter where that was at the time?

Sometimes, I'd travel like that for days, scooting from one part of the country to another, with little more than a smile on my face, and the love of freedom, etched somewhere, deep inside my still beating heart, but most of the time, it was usually around the area that I was living in, or visiting, and perhaps a few of the other towns that were scattered up and down the highway, north, south, east or west.

A lot of that time, was spent with some pretty close friends and associates, who were riding alongside me, or slightly behind, in a well-known formation that was establish almost a half-century before. But there were other times that I can still remember, when I was out there on my own, flying down a road that I never knew existed, let alone, where it would take me to in the end?

Normally, I'd carry a set of handmade, richly-embossed, Italian-leather, saddle-bags, along with a few small but necessary hand tools, a fairly large hunting knife, and at certain times of the year, a somewhat bulky, but still soft and comfortable bed-roll, just in-case I had a reason to pull up along the way. And then of course, there was my favourite little chrome-plated snub-nosed three-fifty-seven magnum, which was small, light and hammerless.

It was a Smith and Wesson, with a smooth, black hand-carved, wooden handle that had the word *Gypsy* etched into the bottom left-hand corner of it, which I carried with me on most of my rides.

It was a gift from a good friend of mine, whose life I had saved one night, from a group of street thugs that were literally kicking the shit out him in an alley way at the time, in a case of mistaken identity I might add, as we both found out at a later date. But it didn't matter about that, he was a friend that needed help, and I just happened to be in the right place, at the right time. They picked on the wrong man that night and it was the wrong time to be messing around like that anyway.

Or perhaps, it was a plain and simple, Army issued Glock, or my old Desert Eagle, that was strapped to my side for good measure, covered-up or concealed, with a tight, smooth, soft leather vest, accompanied by a well-worn, road-beaten jacket, that had two rockers, both above and below a certain well-known, and extremely hard to miss patch, that was centrally located on the back of it, along with tags on the front and down the sides of it as well.

I was the kind of man that usually got his way back then, and I always made damn sure that it showed every chance that I could get. It didn't matter where it was or who I was with at the time. I walked tall, pulled my own weight, had my eyes wide open, kept my back up against the wall, and continuously held my head up high, no matter what? I was living my life to the Hilt. And that was about all there was to that.

I owned some lucrative businesses at the time, which employed dozens of people, on a full-time basis and a few more, on a part-time one as well. I also owned a couple of dozen motorcycles, some pretty fast cars, a few old pick-up trucks and a couple of great RV's, along with several private properties, and some prime commercial real-estate, that were all rented out or leased, and securely handled by a management company that I had also bought shares in, at one time or another.

I owned a restaurant, a night-club, a couple of bars and a gas-station, at one point in time, and I managed to acquire several shares in other corporations that were either up and coming or already established in the world of business and down on Wall Street, but don't get me wrong here, because I certainly wasn't rich by any means, I just had it going on, and I was always hungry for more.

After all, I was fairly intelligent and knowledgeable with it as well. I was young, quick, decisive, intuitive, strong, not bad looking and usually healthy back then, but more to the point, I had always held on to my own no matter what, or where?

Of course, I had partners to contend with as well; who always had their own agendas going on, which usually didn't include mine at all, but that was the price of business back then. It's something that you get use to eventually, something that you truly can't avoid even today, if you really want to get ahead in this life, that is? But all in all, my heart and soul belonged to the open road long before any of that other stuff ever came about.

I was born to it, made from it, carved into and out of it, and I've always sworn that I had at least a million pieces of it, shoved-up underneath my skin, jammed at the back of my throat, crawling up and down both of my legs, and running through every single one of my veins. It was my main addiction, and I always made sure that I owned it, lock, stock and double-barrelled at times.

It's been the air that I breathed, from the moment that I came into this world. It's been the water that I drank, the food that I ate, and the life that I lived, for about as long as I can remember, and there was never any doubt about that. It didn't matter what I was doing at the time, where I was going to, or even who I was with? I was a Nomad and that was undeniably through and through, into the blood, down to the bone, and lived to the Hilt.

I never thought that any of that would change, no matter what I did? But in the end, I was wrong in so many ways, ***dead wrong in-fact.***

****

I'd been the kind of biker that was used to riding up-front and centre, with the rest of the club, riding not too far behind. Plotting the course and setting the pace, for all of the others to keep up with, staying at least two steps ahead of the storms, three, maybe even four steps ahead of our rivals, and then of course, it was five, six, and seven steps ahead of the law, most of the time anyway, but not necessarily in that order, and not always out of harm's way neither, because let's face it, I rode like God looking for Satan most of the time, or at the very least, I rode like Hell looking for Heaven, and I loved every minute of it, maybe even more than I loved life itself?

It was the kind of life, that not many people get to live, and I knew that only too well, in-fact; I was often reminded of it, on a daily basis, by one person or another.

Usually, it was some kind of an idiot of course, some brain-dead little parasite with a death-wish that simply didn't have a fucking clue about much of anything to begin with, thinking the world revolves around them so to speak, and believing that everyone else should cater to that. You know the type of people that I'm talking about? They come in every shape and size that you can think of. But I was a man, caught up in a man's world back then, and most men that I knew, accepted that for what it was, however, there was more than just a few fools that didn't, and they paid a heavy price for their mistakes in one way or another?

It had been one hell of a journey though, that's for sure, wherever it took me and whether or not I had actually wanted to go there in the first place? But it was also the kind of life that most people wouldn't want to live, even if they could, because it was never quite as simple, safe, or secure, as it should have been and at certain points in time, it was always full of problems in one way or another, no matter what I did or what others did along the way. And I know now, that there were too many times, that it should have taken a much better man than me, to actually sort things out. But hey, I've always done what I've had to do, and you definitely can't fault me for that. Or can ya?

I suppose that's why we surround ourselves with the people that we know in the first place?

People that will always have our backs, and then live their lives, the same ways that we live ours, to the Hilt, plain and simple. People, who believe in the club and the some of the same things that we do, like Honour, Integrity, Loyalty and Trust. Because when the shit hits the fan, you're not the only one that's going to catch that splatter, and the more hands that you have with you at the time, the quicker you'll be able to clean up the mess, and then hopefully, move on to better things.

At least that's what you tell yourself, and for awhile, it may be true, but we all know that when it gets right down to it, it's going to be our life that counts the most, to us anyway, no-one else's, then you'll have to do, whatever you have to do, no matter what the consequences are.

That's just the nature of the beast really, or the name of the game if you'd like? It doesn't matter about the people that you may have helped along the way, or how many of them have actually turned around and helped others, if and when they could of course, or even the ones that you've had to hurt in-between times, because that's just the life you live, and you'll need to get your head around that sooner or later, otherwise it'll just drive you mad in the end.

****

Now, the very nature of being a patch-holder, such as an Angel or an Outlaw, a Profit, Joker, or a Priest, or any number of the so-called one-percenters that are out there at any given moment in time, could quickly bring on a slew of negative imagery, combined with some pretty hefty metaphors, to some people's minds at least, that live in today's society, unless they themselves are actually bikers, or at the very minimum, they've known a few bikers in the past.

Usually, the word thug, gang, greaser and criminal, quickly enters into the minds of a lot of people that don't actually ride a motorcycle to begin with, or have never had any real interest in motorcycles in the first place.

However, that's a wrong use of the terminology, and it goes against the very definition of what being a "Real Biker" is all about. Which to be honest; has always been too negative and unjustly promoted as such, through a variety of bought and paid for media outlets, and throughout the course of time.

Fake news, is what it is, and we've all seen it before, no matter what it's about, or even when for that matter? But don't take my word for it. Check it out for yourself.

The fact is; that in a majority of countries and cultures around the world today, you'll find a huge percent of the population, quite familiar with most motorcycles and their riders, and they support that lifestyle, in an assortment of different ways.

Racing for instance, has taken on a phenomenal up-turn, in recent years, with a heavy onslaught of super-bikes, and e-bikes, that have been created by various manufacturers, and the industries behind them.

Every motorcycle out there, has had a team of not only riders, but designers and engineers, they have architects, manufacturers, sales-personnel, assembly-workers and painters, and then there's the mechanics, truck-drivers, transport-managers, cooks, cleaners, hotel chains, along with a variety of clothing accessories etc, all of which, include the general population that's surrounds them, and then goes on to support an even larger lifestyle, that spans from the lowest, to the highest levels, in every society.

Of course, there's the off-road bikes, the scramblers, hill climbers, field and track racers and the tricksters etc, who's owners, simply live for and love to do what they do, always spending huge amounts of time, money and energy doing it.

Motorcycles have taken on the world by storm and some serious stealth, growing more popular, on a yearly basis, with lighter, faster, and larger machines, than ever thought possible before and of course, amongst all of those riders, and all of those workers, there's bound to be a few bad apples kicking around, so to speak, but that's hardly the norm, unless you're a member of an outlaw motorcycle club that is.

Now I'm not saying that all outlaws are bad neither, because you know yourself that we're not. In-fact, you could say that most members of an O.M.C are simply your average type of citizen, underneath their denim and leathers, which typically works from dawn until dusk, raising a family, supporting their lifestyle, and enjoying their freedoms, while being part of the community that they live in as a whole, and that's usually in a good way, but you have to remember that being a member of an O.M.C, also comes with a lot of responsibilities and some of them, won't always be legal, moral, or even righteous at times. No matter how hard we try?

It's the nature of the beast really; and it generally comes with the territory, after all, if you're going to be labelled as an "Outlaw Biker" then you damn well, best be acting like one, because anything less, is just not good enough.

****

Now, if there's one thing that you need to know about this life, then it has to be this. It takes a different kind of person to be a real biker these days, and I reckon that it always has. After all, you don't wake-up early one morning and say, "Hey, I must be a biker" and then run out the door and buy yourself a full-dresser, or some sort of a manic, speed machine, that you can simply scoot on down the road with, faster than stink on shit. And you definitely, don't decide that today of all days, is going to be "the very day" that you're going to change your life forever, no matter what it takes, or what anyone else, has to say about it.

That just ain't a reality my friend, but don't get me wrong here, because we all know that there's a lot of people out there, that really would like to change their lives in some way, shape or form, regardless of how it's done, however, becoming a biker, isn't an option for most of them. In-fact, being a real biker, isn't an option at all.

You don't get to pick and choose this life, instead, it's a life that will always pick and choose you, one way, or another, regardless of whether you like it, or not.

It doesn't matter how much money you have, or even the lack of it, or how much you think you really want this way of life to begin with, or perhaps, you think, that you even deserve it, in some "special" kind of way? But that's not how it is at all, because you simply can't buy this life. It's the one thing that's not for sale. It never has been, and it never will be.

Oh sure, you could always buy the best of the best, if you you're rich enough, that is? You could spend a million dollars, or a million pounds, on just the right machine, sitting way-up high or down so low that your backside is only twenty-plus inches off the ground, mounted on a truly large, quilted, hand-made, Italian leather-saddle, propelled down the road, by an even larger, American made, V-twin engine, with some of the fanciest chromed alloyed wheels that anyone has ever tried to put rubber on. Sporting all of the latest technology, complete with twenty-first century gadgets and some of that fancy Kevlar clothing, right along with some of the best bells and whistles in the whole damn world, but that just ain't where it's at my friend, no, not at all. That's not a real biker, in-fact, it's nowhere near.

That's more like a Klingon, a Poser, or a simple Weekend Warrior type, that's always been, just another Wannabee, no matter what they've done with their lives, or what they think they'd want to do with it? A Wannabee is someone who wants to be something, which they'll usually never be, regardless of what that something, truly is.

They'll try to dress the part, and act the part, and they'll try to convince everyone around them that that's what they really are, but it's easy enough to see through, if you know what to look for, and besides that, if you're a real biker, then you just live the life, twenty-four-seven and three-sixty-five, regardless of what it means, or what other people think it means, at the time.

You throw yourself into it, consistently and constantly, on a daily basis, hour by hour and minute by minute, like a baptism of fire, or perhaps even one that was performed in a Jewish or a Catholic church somewhere, while at the same time, you'll have to remember that real bikers, don't actually do religion in the first place, because their only God, is the club itself, and its church, is a meeting-room somewhere, that's usually located, deep inside the clubhouse walls.

The congregation, if you'd ever want to call them that, is strictly composed of club members, and they are your family members now as well, and the "Word of God" is the ways of the road, the oath to your brotherhood, and the rules of the club itself, no matter what they might be?

It's pretty much, as straightforward as that, because most bikers know what they are, right from the get-go. They know it every single day of their lives, and they simply live it that way, to the Hilt, into the blood and down to the bone. They don't have a choice in the matter, it's already in their character, it's in their make-up, and there's nothing more that they would ever want, except for that, and maybe, just to be left alone to be who and what they already are.

A Klingon, poser or a wannabee, is just another one of those great pretenders of the world, that almost everyone knows and frequently sees, but don't try to kid yourself for a minute, because there's too many of them out there these days, just take a good look around you, especially when the sun is shining, and the weather is warm. But don't get me wrong here, because we all love those weekend-warrior types. They are what truly makes this world go round, and most of them are fairly harmless anyway.

They're the ones, that fire-up their painted steel, highly polished, chromed, rubber mounted, lean machines, early on a Saturday morning, frequently pissing off their neighbours, just in time to scoot on out into the country, far away from all of the hustle and bustle, of their daily little "Straight Citizen" types of lives. But by the end of a Sunday evening, and usually long before the sun goes down, that slick little painted sled, is headed back into the shadows, to be covered in cloth, and bound-up in chains, never to see the light of day again, or at least not until the next Saturday morning that comes around, and only then, if the sun is truly shining.

****

I wasn't that kind of biker though, so this definitely ain't going to be that kind of story. I already knew what I was, long before I ever learned to ride. I grew up with motorcycles, and I got to know some of the men that rode them, at a young and impressionable age.

Most of them were my uncles, cousins, brothers and friends, and whether I was related to them or not, didn't matter at the time and it certainly didn't hurt me any, in the long run.

They were some hard men with soft names, like Mother, Preacher, English, La-Bonk, and Del-Le-Rue. Cowboy, Spider, Wolf, Was, Snake, Bear and Rabbit, and then of course there was Sonny, who just happened to be one of my favourites to begin with, and in-fact; as it turned out, I was actually related to him in a certain kind of way.

There were others of course, like Ted Cotton and Ted Bird, who were definitely brothers from a different mother, and yet they acted like a pair of demented twins when they rode out together, always set on some sort of death and destruction, or hellfire and damnation, for much of the time anyway.

Little-Ginge, Brian Abrahams, Bobby Bolton, Pete the fish, and then of course, there were the dozen or so Dubois brothers, amongst so many of the others, with normal sounding names, that I could never remember them all. But they were just as tough and just as ready as the rest, including my own adopted father way back when, whom they all looked up to at the time, and were only too happy because of him, to take a kid under their wings and teach him everything they knew, about anything at all.

What I learned from them, was a helluva lot, and there's not much doubt about that, although, what I managed to retain through the years, is probably debatable, but hey, I guess I'll just have to keep on living with that.

They all rode hard and fast, they worked hard and long, and they always fought hard, and played even harder, living each moment, day by day and minute by minute, to its fullest, never worrying about tomorrow or what it was, that might just never come, let alone thinking about what the consequences might be, that we'll all have to face in our lives eventually.

Live-free, love-hard, ride-fast, get-rich, or simply die-trying, was pretty much spoken from every man's lips back then, and we continuously took all of that, to the Hilt, with Honesty, Integrity, Loyalty and Trust, and that my friend, was about the way it was when I was coming up in this life, but things change, people change, and the world, well, it keeps on turning, one way or another.

****

10
The Emerald City

Follow the yellow brick road out of L.A, take a sharp turn to the left, and head north into the valley of the damned, which is often referred to as the dead or dying. It's a long trip, filled with all kinds of twists and turns, so you're going to want to bring water with you, or whatever else you'd like to drink, because this journey will definitely take some time to complete and it'll make you thirsty.

When you gaze upon a painted desert that's filled with ten foot tall, three or four branched cacti's without their sombreros on top, you'll need to start your climb up and over the slow rolling hills and high mountain passes, that you'll find along the way, with their large, lush, rich fertile field's of barley, corn, grain and wheat, who's multiple root systems have reached down into ancient glassy sands, along with soft virgin snow-capped mountain peaks, that are covered with some sort of strange and mysterious, other-worldly signs?

Signs, that were once brightly painted on prehistoric, cobbled stone bridges, gigantic monoliths, and towering spires, that reached-up high into the midnight skies, like the fingers of a sleeping giant, all set out in a line that runs over long, crisp and clear, underground fresh-water river-systems, which were undoubtedly carved into this magical land, long before the beginning of man and perhaps the dawn of time.

Still heading North, you'll make your way out past the ancient Redwood forests that always stand-up straight and tall, towards the tattered and slightly twisted Sycamore trees, and the strangely coloured, silver birch ladies, whom, while standing there in their numbers, have had their bark completely stripped from their lower regions, forever scarred in the scratches of the great brown or black-bear's nails, in some sort of weird and sadistically, unanimated fashion, and then you'll head into the midst of the high, but much younger pine forest, that's gently clothed in lichen, surrounded by a dense thicket, wild mushrooms, dark-skinned bluebells and so much more, that no-one could really describe it, or even start to contemplate it all.

Eventually, you'll find yourself beyond the shadows of Mother Nature's last true rainbow. Caught between the wilds of the North Pacific Ocean and those massive eagles nests, that have been carefully built, upon the not so extinct volcanoes, that were once set-out in a ring of fire eons ago, most likely with the help of some long forgotten Deity or Demi-god, whom according to most legends, rode around perched on the back of a strange but colourful demon, or flew up high on the wings of a giant pterodactyl, eventually becoming the father of children, born to the luscious, red-blooded, dark-haired, beautifully fit, young, healthy, and hugely voluptuous, half-human women, that he had always adored and lusted after from a great distance, of course, but could no longer resist when they began to settle into the area, long before the dawn of time and way before the time of man, humankind that is, One-point-fucking-zero, or less?

Perhaps then, if you're truly lucky, you'll eventually come to what's known as the Emerald City, but don't ever expect to find a Wizard there or Dorothy for that matter and all of those little Munchkins, along with the Wicked Witch of the West, either died off, or more than likely, killed off years ago.

****

Of course, if you haven't seen the movie by now, then you probably have no idea of what I'm talking about here, and the words that I've just written, will mean nothing to you at all. But if you have seen it, then you already know that it's a story about a young girl named Dorothy, who bangs her head during a tornado one afternoon while the rest of her family runs for the buried shelter that's dug-out in the bottom of their garden. And as she lays there, completely unconscious, she's rapidly transported into a mystical, far-away land called Oz, where her best friends end up to be her faithful dog named Toto, whom she somehow manages to bring with her, a strange looking, animated scarecrow, that walks, talks and tells her that he's been searching for a brain. A tall and rusty tin-man with an axe, who tells her that he's been looking for a heart and a not so fearsome, cowardly type of weird assed lion that walks upright on his hind-quarters talking to birds, who's apparently been trying to find his courage for the last several years.

Together, they travel the yellow brick road towards the Emerald City, hoping to find a mysterious Wizard, whom they believe, has the power to get the girl safely back home and then give the rest of the group what it is that they truly desire, but first of all, they have to deal with some weird, yet sometimes dangerous scenarios along the way, including the "Wicked Witch of the West" who simply wants to kill them all for no particular reason, along with some of her many minions, who seem only too happy, to do the same.

****

There's other character's in the movie as well, such as the Good Witch and her crew, along with all of the people that actually live in the Emerald City in the first place, but our girl Dorothy, really doesn't know what to make of them all, because they certainly aren't like any of the other people that she's ever met or known before.

Anyway, the girl does eventually return to the land of the living, after saving the day in a variety of Holly-weird ways of course, which include the accidental murder of the Wicked-Witch of the West, along with some of her faithful followers, then she rapidly discovers that all of the characters that were in that far-away place to begin with, were actually real people, living right where she was from in the first place, including the Wicked Witch of the West, her dog Toto, the tin man, the scarecrow and of course that cowardly assed lion.

At the end of it all, she decides that there's no place like home and never sets foot out of the house again, so-to-speak, probably severely traumatized for the rest of her life, for having to go through such an awful experience in the first place.

Still, it's suppose to be one of Hollyweird's greatest movies that was ever made, with record breaking crowds of people, standing in a queue for literally hours at a time, just to get into the movie theatres to see it. But it wasn't for the story that was being told, or even the acting that was done. It was simply because, it was the first movie ever made in Technicolor, which was a feast for human eyes back then, especially when everything else appeared to be plain ole black and white, high upon that silver screen anyway, and I suppose that you could almost say, that we've come a helluva long ways ever since that time, but to tell you the truth, I've often wondered if that's really the case?

****

Now the night-time skies above Seattle, which has always been known as the real Emerald City, long before that movie ever came out, have got to be some of the most stunningly beautiful, spacious, wildly intense and entirely picturesque, that anyone could truly imagine, especially on a warm summers evening, when this medium-sized, high-tech, modern-type super-city, springs into life, with a slightly different view, of what living that life, is all about.

The light pollution doesn't actually allow for star-gazing though, but it is those very lights, that create a certain kind of glow around the city, that shines like no other city in the world, except for maybe Hong Kong, once upon a time, on a cool, bright, crystal-clear night, and I suppose that you could almost say, it really is quite magical, wonderful, strange and perhaps, even somewhat ethereal at certain moments in time, especially when you see it all from a distance.

On a clear day, when you're standing in the right place, you could look west, across a large inland-sea, that's commonly referred to as the Puget Sound and you can gaze upon the snow capped, mountain peaks of the Olympics, that stretch out, in the distance as they lightly shimmer and glisten with the setting sun and yet, in a different location, you could also look to the south and then slowly to the east of the city, where once again, you can gaze upon an inactive volcano, that's called Mount Rainier, which looms larger than life, in what looks to be almost, the exact same distance.

Looking directly east, you'll be able to catch a glimpse of the Rocky Mountains, which actually start-out somewhere south of Mexico City, literally thousands of miles away from Seattle, where they're known as the Sierra Madre and it's from there that they gradually swoop north, through New Mexico, Colorado, Nevada, Wyoming, Idaho and Montana with their foothills steadily rolling all the way up the west coast, and on into British Columbia and Alberta Canada finally ending up in the Yukon and the northern tip of Alaska, somewhere near the Bering Strait. But let's get back to Seattle, before we move on to Alaska.

****

Who could ever forget the Space needle, with its rotating restaurant, high above the land that it was built on? A tall, but simple reminder of the 1962 world's fair that it was originally created for, although it has also become the standard build, for many towers, that have been designed and constructed in much the same way.

Then there's Gasworks Park, Queen Anne hill, and the University district, which has often been home to students, artists, doctors and lawyers, along with so many talented teachers and musicians, that have made their mark upon the world, in one way or another, including Kurt Cobain, Jimi Hendricks, and the Wilson sisters, to name a few.

Off to the west, there's Pikes Place Market, with the smell of freshly caught fish, that lingers through the air, twenty-four-seven and three-sixty-five, and just north of that, the mono-rail system, that runs high above your head, both day and night, no matter what the weather is, or for that matter, any of the multi-storied, air-craft carriers, that usually sit out, on the harbour, always accompanied by a mad array of billion dollar plus, supersized yachts, and some pretty slick, ocean going liners, with their young and gorgeous, bikini clad crews?

On the east-side of the city there's Lake Washington, one the longest, deepest and possibly, the coldest, fresh-water lake on the entire west-coast, crossed by two floating bridges that support super-highways, one of which is interstate 90, which eventually leads you to Snoqualmie Pass and then, on into New York City, some three thousand miles away.

In the north of the city, you'll cross-over the Ballard Bridge, and enter into the Freemont district, or you can travel along the King's highway, which is often called the Pacific Highway in the south, or the King George's

Highway up north, which will eventually lead you into Canada, if you drive far enough, that is.

If you're in a hurry though, there's always the west-coast corridor that parallels the kings highway, from L.A. all the way up to Vancouver B.C., which is known, as I-5, or Interstate Five, and is often the preferred route to travel, for those who don't like travelling alone, or for those, that actually spend their lives travelling alone, transporting goods and equipment, from point A to point B.

In the south of the city, there's Sea/Tac airport where most people fly in to and out of, if they're that way inclined, but there's also a private airport, known as Boeing Field, for the much more sensitive, influential, or extremely rich and elite traveller, which has always been the better way to go, if you could afford it, that is. It's been host to Kings and Queens, along with certain dignitaries, including Senators, and Presidents, which is why it's so special in its own kind of way. That and the fact, that the Boeing Airplane Company, actually own it all, although a lot the land and space, is leased out to the military and the government.

Speaking of military, further south of Seattle, you'll find a city called Tacoma, and south of that, there's McCord Air Force base, which has now been combined with Fort Lewis, one of the largest Army bases in the entire country.

It was home to the 9th Infantry Division and the 272nd Armour division, which could have easily over-seen, a million troops, during the Viet-Nam war, and west of that, there's a large, Trident nuclear submarine base, called Bangor, near a town they call Bremerton, out on the

Kitsap Peninsula, and of course, there's also a massive Coast Guard, National Guard, TSA, FBI and Military Police presence in the area as well.

Interesting enough, there's also a six-thousand, three-hundred square mile Island, that's home to fifteen-hundred incarcerated prisoners, as we speak, most of whom are paedophiles, murderers, rapists and thieves, called McNeil Island, which had its prison system built during the mid 1800's, only to become the largest Island prison in the nation.

Apparently, it also housed Japanese/American citizens, during the Second World War as well, along with all of their families and possible friends, jailed for being a different race and colour, so to speak.

****

If you think about it long enough, you'll begin to realize, that this particular area, is one of the most protected areas in the world, with over ten-million people, spread out, north to south and east to west, all living out their daily lives, while going about their businesses, and that doesn't count the other half of the state in the east, which hosts one of the largest military firing ranges in the world, and a Nuclear storage facility called Hanford, further on up the road near the Tri-cities.

And then there's the 405, a highway that does a soft, semi-circle, around the east side of the Emerald City altogether, for those who don't fancy stopping in town or for the ones that are more comfortable or simply in a hurry to get past the hustle and bustle, that a big city brings.

It'll take you through a little town called Tukwila, which is famous for its "South Centre Mall", one of the largest shopping malls in the area, of course, and then on to Renton, which is another little town, located, just north of the mall. From there you'll drive into Bellevue, where massive computer corporations like Micro-soft and Egghead software or Amazon, have taken over with their giant factories, huge parking lots, and towering high-rise apartment buildings, specifically built to trap, house and contain thousands of their employees, working on the latest computer technologies and the so-called state-of-the-art programs, that they're always trying their best to make us believe, that we can no longer live without, which is typical consumerism at its finest, if you ask me?

Eventually the 405 joins with Interstate five again in the north and you can then carry on all the way to the Canadian border, passing through the country's largest and most colourful poppy field ever been created this side of Afghanistan, located in one of the longest valleys known to man, that was fashioned by an ancient ice-sheet, which melted for mysterious reasons, between twelve and thirteen-thousand years ago, or at least that's what they say?

****

All in all, there's a lifetime of scenery in this area, that no-one could ever cover, no matter which road they took, or how long they travelled it.

From the mountains to the forests, from the rivers to the seas, and all of those little Islands, and back-roads, that lie scattered in-between. It is possibly the most beautiful and diverse State in the Union, barring Alaska of course.

Now the entire U.S. of A is basically riddled with Interstates and their side-roads, just like these, happily making their way from the east to the west and north to south, crossing into one place or another, as if they were part of an interlaced concrete web that was laid out by a gigantic construction spider, all those years ago. They supply the needs of a great nation, spanning from sea to shining sea, as the song says, climbing-up the highest mountains, then dropping down into the lowest valleys in every part of the country that you could imagine, and they are without a doubt, a complete network of skeletons, that hold the very backbone of this country together.

So this is where this part of the story begins, out there on one of those highways, that's not too far from the Emerald City, the Pacific Ocean and Mount Rainier of course, but it ain't about Dorothy, or her dog Toto, and it's a helluva long ways away from Kansas.

****

11
The Edge of the Abyss

I've been a man on a mission for most of my life, but I could never tell you why that is, or what that mission was truly about? It was constantly changing, ebbing with the tide, cresting with the moon, dropping in and out of my crazy little world, like a fresh fallen snow that was scattered on a hill-top somewhere, high-up in the Rocky Mountains perhaps, near Denver, Boulder, or Colorado Springs, or maybe it was way down low along that California coast, somewhere between Salinas and Monterey, out near the Fort Ord Army base, where I did my initial basic training, all those years ago. Or perhaps, it was like some of the people that I've known who were simply here today and gone tomorrow, never to return to what could've, would've, and should've been, in the first place? Who Knows?

It doesn't matter now though, because what's done is done, and what's gone, is gone, and there ain't no going back on any of it, even if you wanted to? But I can assure you this, day in and day out, year after year, here, there, or anywhere, I was doing my thing as usual, and I always did that to the best of my abilities, and you could bet your bottom dollar, that it was continuously to the Hilt.

Then I woke-up one morning and found myself in a completely bizarre situation, that I could never fully explain, nor even start to understand, no matter how hard I tried, and I soon began to realize that it was all over anyway, and whatever the mission had been in the past, really didn't mean a thing to me anymore. In-fact, none of it did. Who would've thought?

****

People say that time, fate and the elements, along with the natural laws of science and physics, all have their ways of catching us up in the end. But I'd been riding that highway to hell and back, from the moment that I took my first breath, long before I could ever walk or talk, and you might just say that there's been some pretty strange, weird, and maybe even wonderful, un-expected and un-natural laws, that were riding right along with me at times, or perhaps, it was one of them, that was driving me along in the first place?

I may never know for sure, because time has a way of doing that, but this is a part of that story, seen through various bits and pieces, of a life that was going places and doing things that not many others, have even dared to dream about.

It was a life, lived to the hilt, with honesty, integrity, loyalty and trust, which is pretty damn important to me as you could probably tell, but more than that, there has been some pretty wild, crazy, and even insane times along the way, and I suppose, if I think about it long enough, there was a lot of dumb-assed luck involved as well. But I don't want to get ahead of myself here, because this entire story has so many twists and turns in it, that it's going to take some time to weave our way through it.

****

It's an incredible sensation, ***waking-up alone***, along the side of an open road, not knowing where you are, or where you've been, at any particular moment in time. Especially during the middle of the night, and in the middle of a work-week as well, but there I was anyway, and all that I could do, was to ask myself, *"What in the hell is going on?"*

As soon as I opened-up my eyes, I was able to take a quick look around, and then realized that I was propped-up against an old guard-rail, running alongside of what appeared to be a very long, dark and lonely stretch, of empty desert highway.

How I got there? Where it was? Or why I was out there to begin with? Didn't even register at the time, and so I just assumed, that I'd been down that road before, and for whatever reasons, I was bound to be down that road again.

Only this time, the trip itself was a lot different to what I'd been used to before, and I know now, that it was one of the most significant turning points of my entire life, up until then at least. In-fact, it was one that I could never have imagined, planned for, or even dreamt about, for that matter.

To start with, I was lost, which was unusual for me, because I had taught myself how to read a map when I was seven years old, and ever since that time, I've made sure to know exactly where I'm at, at any particular moment and in any given situation. I had also spent years in the military, as an M.P. at first, attached to the Airborne Rangers, and then as a Reconnaissance Specialist, in the

Special Forces, or the Green Berets, as they were known back then.

There were a few other things as well, including military intelligence for awhile, jumping out of some perfectly good airplanes at the time, usually just for fun, and only a few thousand feet above the ground, over the jungles of South East Asia at first, and then down to South America afterwards, but hey, that was then and this was now, and to be honest, I hadn't been through any jungles in the last fifteen years or more, except for maybe a concrete jungle that is? But there I was, alone, dazed, confused, somewhat damaged, and completely fucking soaked from a bitter, freezing rain.

Now, blood had been oozing out of an open wound, that was located somewhere at the back of my head, which had trickled itself downwards, eventually sticking to the shirt, jeans and the leather vest, that I was wearing at the time, and then of course, it finally rested into a thick, dark, semi-circle, down along the ground, where I'd been sitting, for who knows how long?

One of my arms felt like it was broken, completely swollen, awkward to move, numb to the touch, and the hand was totally numb as well. My arms, legs and chest, were extremely bruised, cut, scraped and painfully sore, and it felt as if I had cracked some ribs on the right hand side of my chest, making it pretty damn difficult, for me to breathe at the time.

My left thumb was swelled-up to at least two, or even three times its normal size, the skin had split around it, in several different places, and it was still bleeding.

The fingers on the hand, felt as if they had been broken in two, although not nearly as bad as the thumb.

My legs felt like they were on fire, but at the same time, they were as cold as ice, cramping, painful, and it felt like I'd twisted my ankle somehow, making it difficult to use. The foot was swollen, and it was filled with pins and needles, that simply wouldn't quit.

So, I was in a right fucking mess, to put it bluntly, barely alive, hardly aware of my surroundings, and completely caught-up in-between the here and now, and what was obviously becoming a very different, darker and distant future.

My thoughts were running rampant, my heart was racing faster than I had ever known it to race, my eyes were thick and heavy, and my head was pounding like an incessant bloody jack-hammer, that I was sure I could hear somewhere, way-off in the distance.

I began to question everything that I had ever thought about, or even imagined, while at the same time, I was filled–up with more pain and emotion, than I could ever remember, and at the end of it all, I still couldn't figure out why I was out there in the first place? It was an absolute mystery to me? In-fact, my mind was blank, as if it had been shut-down, erased, or maybe something worse, and yet somehow, I knew, deep-down inside, that I had spent my entire life, up to that point anyway, trying to avoid scenarios like this, but I didn't know how, and I didn't know why?

Still, there I was anyway, and all I could do, was assume that at some point in the not too distant past, I must have lost touch with my sanity, or whatever reality, I may have previously known, for whatever reasons, only I simply hadn't realized it yet, nor had I even seen it coming.

I didn't feel that I was prone to that sort of thing though, at least as far as I could tell? After all, they say that insanity runs in families, but I've never had a family to begin with, so that just couldn't be the case.

There had to be another reason behind it all, and what I had to do now, was to find out what that reason was, if I ever got the chance that is?

I had already travelled the world by then, going places and doing things, meeting different types of people, from all walks of life, and then getting to know some of them well enough, to call them my friends, and yet, I had always known where I was, at any given moment in time. In-fact, I had never been lost before, not unless I had really wanted to be lost in the first place, that is.

After all, I had been doing that for years, travelling here, there and everywhere, even going into places where most people would never go, no matter what? Hell, I stowed away on the SS France at twelve years old, not once, but three fucking times. It was my life, it was in the blood, it was in my heart and soul, so to speak, and I was pretty damn good at doing what I did, even if I did say so myself.

I was born to it, at least that's what I've always told myself, but somehow, after all of that, after all the places that I'd been to, and all the people that I had known in this life, I still found myself out there on that fucking highway, wondering what in the world, had really gone wrong?

****

Piss poor planning, you might just say. Reckless behaviour, sudden, or prolonged stupidity, with a capitol S, along with a complete lack of respect, for my own well being, as well as that of any others, that I may have known along the way? Or was it all, actually done by some sort of pre-conceived thought, or design?

Had somebody actually orchestrated all of this? Had I been that stupid to have become the victim of a crime? Or had I simply had an accident that I could no longer remember? Those answers, were completely absent from my mind, at that point in time and all that I could do, was hope that my future would eventually, tell me the tale.

Now, it appeared that the last of my possessions, as meagre as they seemed, had been carelessly, stuffed into a small set of leather saddle bags, that were lying on the ground, spread out, near the bottom of my feet.

Clothing basically, a set of blue denim jeans, an extra long-sleeved Pendleton-type of shirt, some pretty standard black underwear, and a thick pair of winter socks, along with a small cloth bag, that had a few bits of blue coloured stone and some papers in it, which I could barely read at the time.

Apart from that, it seemed like everything else, was simply gone, everything that I could have ever wanted, hoped for or even dreamt of, had simply disappeared, and there was nothing left anymore, not even the memories of a lifetime, that I knew, I must have previously known?

Homeless, penniless and alone, I began searching for the answers to questions that I never knew existed, and if I did, I didn't remember them. Where, when, how and why, became too insignificant to even contemplate, and whatever it was that I needed to search for now, seemed to exist somewhere far beyond the realms of any imagination, reality or comprehension, that I may have had, and yet somehow I knew that it was there, none the less, if I could only find it?

Then, as I sat there watching the rain, turn itself into snow, I started to feel as if I was slipping towards the edge of an unknown abyss, about to be dropped into its dark, frozen, depths, and I suddenly realized, that it didn't matter about the choices that I'd made in this life, whether they were good, bad, or completely indifferent to what other people would actually choose? Because the fact was, knowingly or not, those choices had already been made, regardless of whom it was that might have actually made them. And the consequences of those choices, had led me up to that moment, a moment that was unlike any other moment that I've ever experienced before, or at least, that's what I thought at the time, as I sat there shivering from a bitter cold, harsh and howling winters storm.

****

Now most people would probably say, that I was suffering from some sort of shock and concussion, along with some extreme exposure to the elements, and with a certain amount of damage that was done to the back of my head, which basically, had caused my brain to swell, and in turn, triggered several distinct, and very colourful delusions, that I couldn't control, nor could I have ever imagined, or even started to understand them. And I wouldn't argue too much about that, because in reality, I was simply sitting there alone, at the edge of a dark and empty stretch of highway, watching what was left of my shattered life, quietly fade away, possibly faster than it had ever done before.

However, what I was feeling at that particular moment, and what I was truly going through, were completely different things, and that alone gave me reason to reinforce the belief that I've always had, that there is something more to this life, than most of us, actually realizes? But don't just take my word for that, because it may be the path that I alone have had to take and your own path, as well as others, might actually lead you towards a different destination altogether, who knows?

What I can say, is this. That Abyss, has always been there, lingering, somewhere far beyond the depths of my imagination, or the lack of one, and the real question wasn't whether I was about to fall into it?

No, the real question was more like, "Was I finally making my way out of it?"

The answer remains the same. The truth can never be changed, but I believe it's the perception of that truth, that I've learned to recognize, and perhaps, even more than that, I may have actually come to accept it for what it really is.

What to do with it though? Well, that's just another question, that's been running through my mind ever since, a question that I've been trying to find the answer to, especially after all these years. Writing about these things and telling the world my story, might hold the key, but who really knows, all I can do is try.

****

You see, I never realized, how far that road would take me, or how many years would fly by afterwards, or even where it was that I had already been to in this life, long before that moment ever came about. After all, I was dead to the world at that point in time, and I guess in some ways, ***I've been dead to it ever since.***

****

12
Dead man Riding

When you're dead, you're dead; *it's as simple as that.* You don't know what's up or down, in or out, here, there or anywhere and you really don't care anymore, because nothing seems to matter now, if it ever did? You don't feel, you can't hear, and you definitely won't speak.

Life goes on without you, as if you were never there in the first place and there's nothing you can do about it, even if you wanted to or if you really tried, because the dead are dead. They don't tell tales. They don't lie, they can't steal and they definitely won't cheat.

At least that's what we've all been told in the past, but I can assure you this, that ain't always the way it works, sometimes, there are those clever little clues, along with certain signs and signals, that the dead use to communicate with, and then of course, there are those other times, when the dead, will actually rise-up again, and return to the land of the living, usually with one helluva vengeance.

I know this for a fact, *I've been dead before.*
****
But let me back-up here for a minute, and I'll tell you how I got into this mess in the first place.

It was another time, another place, and a different kind of life, compared to what most people were living back then, but it was never gonna be the way I thought it should have been, no matter how hard I tried to change it.

It was all that I had ever known though, and I had to live with those thoughts on a daily basis, for too many years by then, secretly hoping that things would change themselves. But nothing was ever as simple as that; in-fact, nothing was ever quite the way that I thought it should have been in the first place.

There was always some sort of influence, or some kind of un-seen, or unknown presence, with a hidden agenda, or maybe it was a dark ominous cloud, that was descending over my head, along with an inevitable course of action that I'd have to take, no matter what it cost me and regardless of what I wanted, or at least what I thought I wanted at the time?

After all, it had been that way for my entire life, and I guess that I just figured that that's what had gotten me down the road this far to begin with. So, I wasn't about to stop it now, even if I could?

****

I took a long look around, as I left the club that night, almost as if I was looking at it, for the very last time. I remember seeing a young heavy-set prospect, with a shaved-head, different coloured eyes, a dangly earring, tight, worn-out, old blue jeans, and some sort of crazy looking birthmark, or a tattoo that appeared to be travelling up and down the side of his face, then rapidly disappearing underneath his collar, that I had never noticed before.

A newbie I assumed, standing outside, smoking a cigarette, alone in the shadows, near the end of the building, watching over the motorcycles that were all lined-up in a row, with their heavy ass-ends, tucked-up tightly against the southern wall.

The kid had nodded his head in my direction, as I made it through the door, so again, I just assumed that he knew who I was, although thinking back on it later, I wasn't so sure? After all, he could have been anybody really?

He was a single, dark, solitary figure, out there on his own, standing underneath a moonlit sky, watching over a half-a million dollars worth of G.A.M.C. machinery, as if his very life depended on it, which to be quite honest, it probably did?

Let's face it; bikers can be pretty damn precious about their machines. I know this to be a fact, because I always have been and I guess I always will be.

I also noticed a couple of love-birds that were sitting in the cab of their pick-up truck, that was parked-up near the corner of the lot, with its engine still running, sucking face with each other, entangled in naked arms and legs at the time, totally oblivious to the outside world, and without a care or a worry, about who could actually see them sitting there.

Then I noticed the two tractor-trailers, which were parked-up just outside the hotel rooms which were further across the lot, one was a dark-red, bull-nosed Peterbuilt, and the other some kind of fancy KW cab-over, if I remember right?

There were three more without their trailers, parked head to toe further out on the road as well; all five of the hotel rooms were booked as usual. Business was good.

It was easy money really, and the girls who worked it, were always kept happy, healthy, safe, and secure. After all, the restaurant was open twenty-four-seven, three-sixty-five, and every one of the hotel rooms, had a hidden panic button, that went straight to security, if trouble ever happened?

I had always run a tight ship, and I've never liked stupid people, so if any punter got out of hand, they got tossed quicker than what they knew had hit em, and if they didn't like that, or if they were simply too much trouble to begin with, then they were quickly eighty-sixed for life, never to return.

Anyway, all of that was before I started-up my bike, kicked it into gear, twisted the throttle, and then finally roared off, out of the parking lot and into the middle of the night, like a mad-man on a mission, out for one last and final ride.

Of course I didn't know that yet, but I swear I could feel it coming anyway, like a bad omen around my neck, pounding me to the ground, tearing me up inside, and trying to smash the life right out of me. It was a moment caught-up between what was already, and what was yet to come. But again, I didn't know that? I didn't know that I was a dead-man riding that night, nor did I ever think it would happen so fast?

I suppose that we never do in the grand scheme of things, not until it hits you in the face that is, like some bloody random brick, that's been thrown off an overpass in the middle of nowhere, and by then it's too late to do anything about it anyway, because the damage has already been done.

Assassins, they're always out to get you, and it doesn't matter who you think you are, or where you're at, at the time? They're out there anyway, especially when you least expect em, when you can't out run em, or hide from em, and usually when you don't even know where you are, or where they're at?

That's when they like to strike though and that's just the plain and simple truth of it all. I've had my run-ins with them before, and it ain't too funny I can tell ya, but they haven't got the best of me yet, and hopefully they never will.

****

It was raining that night, who would've thought? Bloody winter showers and all of that, but I really didn't mind the rain that much, I never have.

A little bit of rain has typically kept me more alert, even more alive, than what I usually felt, besides that, the rain has always cleaned-up the air around me, as well as the roads that were laid out in front of me, but most of all, I loved the smell of it, especially when I'm scooting down the highway without a care in the world, alone, relaxed and usually, deep into some sort of restful, or maybe even peaceful thought process at the time.

Now, the meeting that I had just come from had ended fairly abruptly, leaving me with a strong, sharp, twisted, type of feeling that was sitting there, like a lump of hot coal, searing me down to the bone, somewhere near the pit of my stomach.

Something was wrong, that's for sure, but I couldn't quite put my finger on it and I couldn't quite get my head around it neither, which is fairly unusual for me, because I've always been the kind of guy to stay focused, especially when others couldn't. I suppose that my Army days might have taught me that?

There was a war about to take place, and I was caught-up in the middle of it, no matter what I had to say about it, or what I could actually do to try and prevent it from happening to begin with. And I certainly didn't like that much, not one bit. But I also knew that I didn't have a choice in the matter. Too many things had happened for any of it, to stop now. Blood had been spilt, sides had been chosen, and the life that I've always known, was about to come to a sudden, final and fatal conclusion.

Something that no-one would've seen coming, in a month of Sundays. Or maybe I did, but I just didn't want to think about it at the time.

Normally, a meeting at the Desert Rose Inn was a little more relaxed, even laid back most of the time. After all, it was an amazing bar to go to, with great food, good looking waitresses, intelligent bar-keeps, and some pretty good entertainment from time to time as well, world class even, if I do say so myself. But that night had been strictly business, and as usual, business was booming.

Twenty-five or thirty puppets, five strikers, an accountant, a couple of sergeants, three captains, a half-dozen associates, a V.P. (vice-president) and another twenty-five so-called, friends of friends, along with yours truly of course.

All meeting over what was yet to come, what was already, and what should and shouldn't be, at least to their way of thinking, but not necessarily mine.

It wasn't bad for the middle of the week though, but I also knew that it was all going to hell in a bucket, no matter what was said or done, and that really isn't a good feeling let me tell ya, no matter who you think you are?

Now, it didn't take a genius to know, that once gambling was opened up to the public, serious money and even more serious players, would be crawling out of the wood-work, looking for their piece of that proverbial pie, so to speak. And with the new hi-tech machines, that were brought into play at all the local establishments, it was only a matter of time really, to see who controlled the most, and then to figure out, who it was that was actually, the most in control.

Drugs, prostitution, loan-sharking, certain goods and services, and of course, different kinds of personal protection, had always been the main-stay for most bikers through-out the years, and investing those funds into a so-called, legitimate business, wasn't an easy thing to do, but the talent had always been there for me and I had managed to do quite well, for what seemed to be a fairly long period of time.

Change was coming though, all in the form of legalized gambling, Government backed and sponsored, and of course, it was opened-up to just about anyone that had the coin to compete, and you could bet, that there were way too many of those.

Rich kids mostly, with their Daddies trust-fund accounts, that really didn't know their asses from a hole in the ground to begin with, and they certainly had no idea about what to spend that money on. But there were others as well, and some of them were pretty serious players, with old style finances, along with older family traditions and beliefs, as well as numerous connections, that were well protected, with a lot of old style muscle, and the right kind of modern day machinery behind them.

People like the Irish, Mexicans, the Italians, or the Chinese/Japanese types, which were old school, old families, old friends and definitely old money.

The machines weren't cheap to begin with, because the government controlled that aspect of things. You could easily say goodbye to thirty-five percent of your money, right then and there.

Licensing wasn't cheap, and the location rental was never cheap either, unless you already owned the property of course, which was always in demand, and it was all too limited as well. Federal regulations saw to that. You could put three or four machines in here and there, but you couldn't have seven in the same place, or you could have a whole building full of machines, just as long as the payouts were only a quarter of what the regular payouts were.

Payouts were maxed at a thousand dollars in this State, which was hardly worth the effort, or so I thought. After all, you could ride down to Vegas in less than twenty four hours and win yourself a cool million dollars with the single flip of a coin there. If you were lucky enough, that is? But the way the "Man" wanted this to work, was definitely penny on the dollar stuff, and it would take a lot of hard graft to make any real profit from it, even if the larger payouts, were only an average of one, in every three or four thousand.

I didn't like any of it and I argued through the night about it all. On the one side, I could see the long-term investment that was being laid out. Sure, five or ten years down the road, and maybe it would pay for itself, eventually. If everything went well enough that is?

But on the other side of the coin, there was also that immediate little cash crunch, or should I say, five million little cash crunches to be exact, and each one of them, with its own name, rank, and serial number, and the worst part about the whole deal, was the locations.

The best locations for something like this, was going to be with the "Neveau Riche." Five-star establishments, places of the rich and famous. Places that were already held by more money, than you could ever shake a stick at and a hell of a lot more influence than what most bikers had ever dared to dream about, and of course, above and beyond all of that, was the absolute power aspect, a power, that could never be bought or sold, for neither love nor money, because it was already owned, operated and controlled, by a certain select and shall we say, nameless few.

People, that could make you disappear forever, without a single trace, and wipe your very existence off the face of the planet at the same time, as if you had never been born in the first place.

Definitely not the biker bars, titty clubs, or even whorehouses, but hey, the "friends of friends" didn't quite see it the same way as I did and all I could do, was wonder why that was?

It wasn't like they were stupid, ignorant, or even asking for a hand out, in-fact, nothing even close to that, because they already had the cash to splash, and they were always looking to invest their money into something new. That's just what they did and there was never any doubt about that. But what they were after this time around was a double-up. Matching funds, along with an equal partnership in the club itself, which of course, was something that I'd never consider doing in the first place, and as it happens, the anti for all of that on my side, was over Two and a half million dollars, which to them was merely peanuts at the time, but certainly not to me.

Right now, was definitely not the time for any of this to happen, to say the least? The **"Bandaleros"** were on the move as usual, and they were pushing the **"Road Kings"** right along with them.

They were two of the largest motorcycle clubs in the world now, and of course, each one had to be bigger, better, badder, and a lot stronger, than the other one had ever thought about being, and they weren't messing around with that.

The war in the east had turned bloody, and it had been going on for far too long. Regular citizens were affected; innocent people were getting in the way, some of them had been maimed or killed and of course the media was involved, pushing it out on the nightly news, squawking about it on the radio, and then writing it down in the daily papers.

So it was no surprise that the governments on both sides of both borders, started drafting new laws to outright ban, or at least stop motorcycle clubs altogether.

Business was slowing down in the east, which had a knock-on effect for the rest of the country, and eventually, the rest of the world. In-fact, whole industries were drying up, and people were running scared, the federal noose was tightening around them and it certainly didn't feel good to anyone at the time.

I'd seen it happen before, back in the late seventies, and the early eighties. Entire clubs had been wiped out; Montreal was one of the worst, with over a hundred and fifty bikers from the Satan's Soldiers Motorcycle Club, who were kidnapped, killed, jailed, hospitalized, or had simply disappeared in one way or another. Who knows what really happened to them all?

It was even rumoured at the time that "Mother Meckuen," the president of the main chapter, had had his head cut off and then delivered to his wife in a pretty little, plastic lined, cardboard box, complete with a bow, and a greeting card, just in time for Valentine's Day.

Now, I ask you, who in the hell does that kind of shit? Nobody in their right mind, surely? No-one could be that sick, twisted, demented or fucking depraved.

Anyway, it was a mess to say the least. No-one knew which way to go from there, or even whom to trust after that, for way too many years afterwards, and it affected far too many people, including some of those that I personally knew at the time.

It was business sure enough, but at that particular point in time, it wasn't any of my business, so I never let it bother me, although I'll always remember it, like it was yesterday and for me, yesterday was bad enough.

****

In the south, one of my chapters, **Rebel's Crew**, had just got hit pretty badly, and the reasons behind it, wasn't really known yet.

Rebel was all right, but three of his younger sergeants were dead, a half-a-dozen righteous rides were completely trashed and of course, the clubhouse, which they had only just rebuilt that spring, had been blown-up again, and as you would imagine, business there, had stopped altogether, thanks to the local constabulary and the feds of course, even though they weren't so sure who was involved at the moment neither, since no-one was really talking and again, no-one saw anything anyway, because they never do, and who could blame them for that?

I had an idea about it though and I knew that it wouldn't be too long before the truth came out. Shit like that never stays a secret for long anyway. It was only a matter of time really, and I had lots of that.

I had also made a call as soon as I found out about it, and I knew that if there was one thing that the guy on the other end of that telephone line was really good at doing, it was hunting people like this, just as quickly as he could. Which was never too long in the grand scheme of things? No matter where they ran, or where they tried to hide. Still, things had been pretty good for a long time by then; there hadn't been a killing in my ranks for the last three or four years, up until that point in time anyway, and I was pretty damn proud of that, after all, my boys were well-known to be the best of the best, but it had been a long time coming and like a slow moving storm, it would carry on out of control, probably for a long time to come. Unfortunately, things like that, usually do.

So no, it didn't make any sense to me, to invest into this new agenda that they'd been talking about. That money was needed for other things, and that was the way that it had to be.

It didn't matter who liked it or not, because this was business plain and simple and this particular business was mine. I just had to hold on to it, and then stand my ground as usual. Who would've thought?

****

It didn't take me long to find the highway home that night. After all, I had made the same trip on a regular basis for the last couple of years or maybe more.

It was my M.C. as well as my nightclub, which I owned outright, lock, stock, and barrel as they say, along with a few personal investors, and the bank of course, and I had always made sure that things were running just as smoothly as possible, even if that meant making several daily visits, or the odd night-time one as well, like the one that I had just made. It didn't matter which it was, it had to be done regardless, and I was the only one that could really do that.

The rain had finally stopped falling, just a few miles into my ride, and the throttle was cranked wide open by then.

The roads were drying out, and I loved the feel of the wind rushing towards my face. That's what I lived for most of the time, the simple thrill of the ride.

The rest of it didn't matter at all, but out there, I could fly and that's exactly what I needed to do right now, I needed to fly. I needed to fly as high and as far, and as fast, as I could possibly go, because time wasn't waiting for me, or anyone else for that matter. It never does, it never has, and it never will.

The wind screamed in my ears, when I reached that hundred-mile an hour mark. One-ten, one-twenty, and if I could, I'd make time slow right down, stop it, or even spin it around awhile, and what was yesterday, would now become tomorrow. But of course, I knew that I couldn't do that sort of thing, not a chance in hell.

I don't know why, but for some reason, I started thinking back through all of the years, remembering the good times and some of the bad, as I gently pushed my custom painted, fairly new, modern day, steel horse, in and out of the curves that were consistently laid out in front of me.

Someone had done an amazing job designing that highway, putting all the right cambers in all the right places, cutting through the scenery at the right time, taking it down through the valley along the river, and then a gentle climb back-up to the top, with a few hair pin turns, and the odd ridgeback thrown in along the way.

It was a good ride; it always has been, almost as good as that coastal highway down in Southern Cal, which is still one of my all time favourites.

The sun, the sea and the sand, along with a great biker's bar, that was called the Silver Moon, back in the day. You couldn't beat that, no matter where you went. In-fact, that's one of the reasons that I bought the Desert Rose to begin with; it had the same sort of feel about it. Almost like coming home, not just for me, but for everyone else as well. It was a great place to be, that's for sure.

My mind drifted backwards even further in time. I hated it, but I couldn't stop it. Those memories were rearing their ugly head, and there wasn't much that I could do about it.

Growing up in the fifties hadn't been that bad really. Sure, I lived through a lot of heartache and pain back then, but who hadn't?

I got through it, as we all do. I survived it in the best ways that I knew how and whatever it was that might have hurt me in the past, had just become part of the fabric that had made me stronger in the long run.

It was the iron in my armour, so to speak; a little rusty now perhaps, slightly bent and out of shape in places, possibly even non-existent in others, but still, it was that, that was keeping me protected, even after all these years.

I remember the Chevy's and the Hot-rod Lincoln's of my youth. The fancy Ford coupe's and those crazy-assed, low-riding Cadillac's along with the pretty bottom Mercury's that cruised up and down the strip, half-way out on main street, almost every Friday and Saturday night, with their horns honking, their lights flashing and their radios blaring out just as loud as they could get.

All of them with young assed drivers, that were out to pick-up every good looking woman in sight, as they slowly drove past them, travelling at no more than five or six miles an hour, consistently watching all the girls who were huddled together down on the street corners, that were talking amongst themselves, usually about what they were wearing at the time, or who's boyfriend had the finest car, the most money, the fanciest house and probably the biggest dick.

I also remembered watching those girls myself, as they waited around for the Cadillac's to drive by, with their brushed velvet seats, fancy paint jobs, chromed wire rims, and convertible rag tops, which of course, only the richest boys in town could actually afford to drive in the first place. But the best of the best, was that powdered blue and white, fifty-five T-bird, and of course, the red and white, nineteen fifty-three Corvette, that one of my uncles, happened to own.

They were both kept in perfect showroom condition, all the way up from Flint Michigan and Chicago Illinois originally, but they were hardly driven anywhere else, unless of course, it was out on a clear summer's evening, with the moon shining bright and some gorgeous, young, big breasted, little honey, sitting in the passenger seat, with her pretty long legs, slightly opened and her skirt, pulled-up high, and you just knew that she was definitely not into driving too far away from where those cars were actually stored to begin with.

Yeah, my uncle was a pretty lucky guy back then, until the war took him that is. He made it home alright, but he could never drive those cars again, a chopper crash near the

DMZ, and then a sniper round that took out the lower part of his spine, making his legs completely useless.

In the end, he sold those cars, wheeled himself out to the garage afterwards, and then put a bullet into the side of his own head. Shame really, he was such a sweet guy, one of my favourites.

I still remember the Bobby socks and the pigtails that some of the girls wore back then, with their super tight, button-down blouses, extra large breasts, hard, lengthy nipples, and smooth, three-quarter length, pleated skirts, while at the same time, they'd be wearing that dark, glossy red, Marilyn Monroe, type of lipstick, with a heavy blush and foundation, green or blue eye shadow, and of course, they all had a smile for every good looking guy that came their way, including me most of the time, even though I was still a baby compared to the rest of them. Well maybe not all the rest, but you know what I mean?

You weren't anyone, unless you had three or four of those sweet babes, riding right along with you, in your brand new Cadillac convertible, driving it just as slowly as you could, around the circuit throughout the night.

Bikers had never been counted for much with that crowd back then, and in-fact, they still aren't. Four wheels are usually considered to be much better than two and a whole lot safer to most people anyway. But that had never put me off, after all, I was more than just a biker, I had a little bit of class going on, at least that's what I always told myself.

I remember burger joints and the drive-in movie theatres, root-beer and roller-skates, street-rods, raisers, and ice-cream parlours, and then of course, I'll always remember my love for the motorcycles.

American made, American strong, with a machine like that, you could never go wrong. Which even back then, was just your typical, mindless, commercial bullshit of the times? It was thrown out on the telly and in the theatres, which I suppose, is no different than today really? Never mind, it definitely worked, that's for sure.

I remember the blue jeans and black leather jackets that I still wear even now, after all these years, as well as the smell of burning rubber in the air, and high octane gasoline, which usually got splashed onto my boots, jeans or leather jacket.

I remember long roads, clear-skies, and mile after mile of used-up old Tar-Mac that always took me to where I wanted to go and a lot of the time, where I had never been to before, but that was the way it was back then, Heaven on Earth, you might just say, at least for a biker anyway.

So yeah, growing up in fifties was just as good as any other time I figured, maybe even better than the rest, but you never know that for sure? Because things change, people change and before you know it, we've gotten a whole lot little older, if we're lucky that is?

I began thinking about what it was, that actually made me the way I am? What was it that led me down this road to begin with, and what had really brought me through it all? Was it my birth mother, or the woman who was gone before I turned three, or my father, who had died at my birth?

Maybe it was my adopted parents that split up when I was five, forcing me to go through children's homes and foster parents, with sick and twisted, wannabe mother and father types, which led me to the streets, and then eventually the jails that I found myself in, right before they shipped me off to Viet-Nam?

Of course, some people say, that it was the war itself, or that it was the memories of seeing a few of my closest friends at the time, shot, stabbed or completely blown to pieces right in front of my eyes, or maybe it was the twenty-plus years of constant, bloody turmoil, that I'd been living through ever since?

Some people say I was a hero back then, apparently more than a few times during my tours over there. Gaining a Bronze Star, a Purple Heart, and a couple of other medals for some sort of bravery, or so-called exceptional distinction? But who really knows for sure?

I can barely remember it now, three frigging tours over there, and they're all just a bloody blur really? It's pretty strange how the mind works, and it's not really funny how that time has been simply been blanked out. Oh well.

To be honest here, I was just doing what I had to do to keep myself alive, which is something that soldiers, aren't supposed to do in the first place?

They're supposed to die for their country and all of that. So you can believe me when I say, that I was more than a little surprised, when I finally did return back home. But now, I felt nothing really, in-fact less than nothing most of the time, if that was even possible?

Instead of feeling like some sort of a hero, I felt more like a villain. One that was stuck-out somewhere, in another dimension perhaps, or another place in time, and there was always another endless bloody war, no matter where or what?

I didn't like that feeling at all, not one fucking bit. But hey, that was my life, take it or leave it, it was all that I had, whether I wanted it or not, never mattered?

In-fact, that's all that we ever have, so we make the most of it, because when it's over, it's just fucking over, and there ain't no coming back from that, at least that's what I used to think?

Never mind though, life has never been too easy to begin with, and if it ever was, it probably wouldn't be worth living it anyway. Too damn boring I'd have to say, and let's face, what doesn't kill you, just makes you stronger, or so they say? Whoever they really are?

I was lucky with that kind of thing, because I was never bored for very long; I just wasn't that type of guy. I always had something going on, something that I needed to do, or some place that I needed to go, and there was always someone else to see, day or night, week after week, it didn't matter when, or where it was. If I was needed, I was there. That's just the way things were, and you can bet that I loved every minute of it, at least most of the minutes that I didn't actually hate.

So, none of the past mattered to me now, because it was all just slivers of some distant, faded, memories, that were comprised of way too much bullshit, that I had to go through, and didn't want to keep in the first place. In-fact, the sooner they disappeared, the better off I'd be, as far as I was concerned, because everything that I've ever lived through, had only made me stronger.

Everything I've ever been through, had simply become a part of what I was, who I was, how I was, and how I'd always be, even though, it was never by choice, you understand, because most of the time, it was like sheer fucking necessity, or perhaps some sort of providence, or maybe even karma, built-up from another life?

I was a soldier, a prophet, an engine poet and a brother to the sun, but more than that, I was an Angel, and there was no doubt about that, because I was born to it, brought-up in it, lived with it, and I'd probably die from it in the end.

I guess that I figured, that that was about all there was to that, whether I ever wanted it or not, never became a question in my mind. It was all that I had, all that I had ever had, and I held on to it, no matter what.

My life had been lived on the edge of an unknown abyss, standing at a point, that was fixed somewhere between a colourful, yet somewhat ghostly sort of light, and some really dark, powerful forces, that were always more than what anyone truly knew?

One day, I'd fall to one side of it or the other, but the next day, I'd get back up again, and then I'd jump to the opposite side, which is not much more than what a mountain climber does really, at least that's what I had always told myself.

Every day was different, that's the way it was. That's the way it had always been and that's the way I liked it. After all, I was pretty much used to that, and perhaps I figured that it was the only way to be, for me anyway? Regardless of what I wanted, or what I thought I wanted at the time?

****

It was right about then, that all of a sudden, and out of the darkness, a massive bright flash appeared on both sides of my mirrors at exactly the same time, almost blinding me on my ride. It was like the heavens had opened-up, turning the night into the day, in less than a heart-beat, and sending a shiver up and down my spine that I couldn't possibly begin to describe. Something had exploded into a massive fireball, something, somewhere, way-off into the distance that was behind me now, way-back from where I had just come from. I couldn't tell what it was yet, but whatever it was, it was huge and it had lit up the sky like a tomahawk cruise missile that had just hit a fuel depot, somewhere near the southern border of Iraq and Kuwait. Somewhere, around the Persian gulf, as you might imagine?

My first thought was a plane crash, or a meteorite, that had fallen out of the sky, but of course I know better now, it was something completely different to any of that. I also know that I should have stopped right then and there, but I didn't, and I should have slowed down a bit, and maybe even turned around to check it all out properly, but I didn't.

I was in the zone by then; really enjoying my nights ride out, scooting along, into the country, without a care in the world, and let's face it; it wasn't any of my business anyway, so it wasn't any of my concern, or was it?

Oh shit, who put that fucking truck there?

****

Postscript

If you ever hit something on a motorcycle, with the throttle wide open, and you just happen to be up and over that hundred mile an hour mark at the time, then you could pretty well guarantee that you're screwed and about as close to being dead as dead can get, which is undoubtedly the best word to use in that kind of situation. Dead that is.

After all, the bike you were riding is suddenly trashed so far beyond recognition that it would be impossible to salvage any of its parts, or even identify the ones that were left. It would be completely broken, bent and twisted, so far out of shape that you could never use any part of it again, with its bits and pieces, thrown here, there and everywhere, which would take days and weeks to finally find, let alone, sort them all out.

Some of which, may have even become a part of what it was that you actually hit to begin with and some of those other bits and pieces, might have even become part of you, turning you into a form of twisted steel, in every aspect of the word and its meaning. But regardless of that, everything about that bike and you, has suddenly been wrenched in ways that you could never imagine, let alone describe, and every little bone inside your body, suddenly feels as if it's just been smashed into a million pieces, whether it has or not? And if you're lucky, and I do mean lucky, then nothing works at all.

Your mind, your body, in-fact your entire being just stops, and then it starts to go numb as you find yourself thrown into that big black hole that's been filled-up with nothing more than emptiness.

****

Before any of that happens though, you'll remember everything you've ever said, done, and lived through in life, the good, the bad, and every bit of the fucking ugly that you've ever known, or tried to know, or imagined, no matter how small and insignificant that may have been at the time. And no matter who you think you are, or who you were, and there ain't no getting out of it, trust me, everyone pays for their sins eventually.

It's a feeling that we'll all have, at some point in our lives, I can guarantee it, but some of us, will get there a little faster than others, and some of us, might even come back to tell the tale.

****

13
Recollections

My first recollection*, *was when I was little more or less than a year old, standing alone in an empty kitchen, wearing nothing but a raggedy old diaper and a cute little smile upon my face, inquisitively gazing upwards towards a saucepan that was half-filled with cooking-oil, which was sitting in the middle of an open flame, on top of what appeared to be a very large gas or wood burning stove that I could barely reach at the time. Of course, the cooker wasn't that big at all really, it's just that I was a baby back then and everything around me had the appearance of being much larger than what it truly was.

What caused me to reach-up for the handle when I did? I guess I'll never know for sure? Simple curiosity I'd imagine, or maybe I was hungry at the time? But regardless of any reason, it was that very moment that changed my life forever.

That one single moment, opened my mind to all of the pain, horror and heartache that this world has to offer and it showed me just how fragile life would truly be.

And it happened in nothing more than a blink of a young boy's eye. A trauma so painful, that I'd never forget it, no matter how hard I tried. In-fact, I still carry the scars of that burning oil, which splashed itself all over my head, hand, arm and body, while at the same time; it seared the skin that it touched, down to the bone, suddenly throwing me into a dark, deep abyss, filled with absolutely nothing but emptiness, caressed by heartache and despair, an abyss that I've had to constantly fight with, my entire life…..Disconnect.

****

I remember the pain and agony that I felt all those years ago, the damage that it caused and the sudden effect that it had, not just for me but for some of those around me as well. I remember the flames as they quickly spread across the floor and started rising up the wall. I remember the rotten smell of smoke, as it filled-up the room, which rapidly became too thick to see through, and I remember the intense heat of it all, as the air was being sucked out of my tiny lungs.

I remember how small and utterly insignificant I was at the time, how helplessly alone, afraid and utterly horrified I became afterwards. I remember the burning of my hand, the searing pain, the rancid smell of hot, crisp, smouldering bacon, that wafted its way upwards into my nostrils, and I remember the deep, dark, icy-cold emptiness, that suddenly came right along with it.

But most of all, I remember that old man, with long, flowing white hair, different coloured eyes, and a lengthy scar on his face, picking me up and taken outside the burning building, and then the darkness that came with it as well, that immediate loss of sight, sound, and senses, along with any real reason that there may have been for what had just happened to me.

That darkness kept me living in fear, for months, if not years on end afterwards. That same darkness that seemed to surround and envelope me, as if it was some sort of rough, ragged, used-up, worn-out, old riding blanket, that had been tossed into the corner of an abandoned stable for practically decades at a time. That very same darkness, that I could never rise above and never quite breathe through, because of how thick, dirty and dusty it tasted, and I could never quite see through it neither, no matter how hard I tried.

I could never walk around it, I could never talk above it and I could never see anything beyond it, because of all the visions that I had, along with my own silent, internal screams, that were left reverberating around inside of my head, which never truly stopped, full of unimaginable terrors that I could never hope to control nor even comprehend at the time and they were more than just a little deafening, let me tell you, they were like a freight train crashing into a station, at the end of the line, that was going a hundred miles an hour. Everything around me had suddenly changed in less than a heartbeat and I didn't know why?

That one little moment in time however, drove out all that I had accomplished up to that point in my life, which to be fair, wasn't a lot in the grand scheme of things, after all, I was just a baby, but it would take me literally years before I could start over again. In-fact, that one, tragic little moment, eventually triggered an entire succession of other tragic moments in my life that I thought would never end.

Defining moments that were stretched out over decades of time and literally miles upon miles, of empty space, without any rhyme or reason behind them at all? At least none that I could ever hope to understand or even imagine?

Definitive moments, that I never had a choice over, nor did I have any say in the matter what-so-ever and yet, there they were anyway and I had to deal with each and every one of them, in the best ways that I could, which may not have always been the right way to do things, as far as anyone else was concerned that is, but I'm quite sure that it wasn't always the wrong way neither, and besides that, when it really gets down to it, we're all going to do, whatever we have to do, when we have to do it. So in the end, I guess that's exactly what I did, regardless of any rhyme or reason that anyone could ever put behind it and regardless of what it cost me in the long run.

****

Now, you might just say, that my life started out on that open road to begin with, and to be quite honest, I used to tell people that I was born on the back of that old motorcycle, headed down south along highway one, somewhere in-between Frisco and L.A.

My mother had always told me that she had wished she had dropped me instead of that damned bike and of course, I've agreed with that, because I knew that I'd been on one hell of a ride ever since, no matter where it took me and whether or not I actually wanted to go there in the first place? But the truth of the matter is, I never knew my mother, she died the night of my birth, and I was born thousands of miles from that California sun, along with its soft, warm, welcoming sands, as well as that long, beautiful coastal highway that I've always loved to ride, and even though I enjoyed the entire state just as much, for most of the time anyway, it would take four years to get there and another twenty-plus years or more, before I finally called it home and even then, it was only for a little while.

My life clicked-up the miles though, right from the get-go. Eight-thousand of them, by the time I reached two years old, another six-thousand miles, by the time I turned four and then another ten-thousand miles, before I reached the age of six, and all of that, was during a time when most people considered themselves more than a little lucky to be able to travel twenty or thirty blocks, during the course of their entire lives. In-fact, some people still live their lives that way today, whether they actually need to or not, although many of them will travel abroad, at least once or twice a year, for some kind of holiday, if nothing else.

Now most of those miles that I travelled back then, wasn't actually done on the back of a motorcycle, because there were always planes, trains and automobiles involved, which usually took me from point A to point B, a helluva lot faster than any two-wheeler could. Besides that, motorcycles weren't much more than bone-shakers, ass-breakers or flat-out widow-makers, in more ways than you could ever count and the truth of the matter is that they're not much different today.

They were usually light-weight, solo rider types, with small single or double piston engines that were generally built for speed more than actual comfort and they definitely weren't built for a twenty-four-thousand mile road trip, no matter what the manufacturers had to say. But regardless of that, it was the smell of old motor oil and used-up engine grease, dead-flies, stink-bugs and burning bits of rubber, that was casually mixed in with human sweat, hot leather-jackets, raggedy old blue-jeans and cheap-ass gasoline, that evaporated during the heat of a long, summer's afternoon, with the hint of a hard rain coming down somewhere, way off in the distance, along with that constant hum of a large V-twin engine, filling up my ears and reverberating around inside the depths of my soul, that were without-a-doubt amongst some of the sweetest memories that I knew at the time, and definitely at the beginning of all of the recollections, that I actually had of this life.

A shrink would call them triggers in my later years, simple little things really, that took me back through the pages of both space and time, like a book that wasn't quite written yet. But to me, there was never any doubt about it, it was the lure of the open road, with the wind rushing through my hair and the sun rising high above me, shining down upon my skin that was unquestionably in my blood by the time I was born, and that's about all there was to that.

Maybe it was there before I was thought of, maybe it was there in my father's life perhaps? Who knows for sure? It certainly has made me wonder at times though and I guess that's just the plain, simple truth of it all.

Still, there were a lot of stories that were told about it all, at different times of course, by different people, throughout the years. But no-one knows who or what to believe there? Contradiction after contradiction, with nothing ever adding up and I was sure that most of it was lies anyway, because people just love to talk don't they?

It had even been suggested that I was kidnapped as a baby, stolen from my real parents, held for ransom maybe? And that the children's home that I was adopted out of, the first time around that is, was in on the whole damn thing?

After all, stealing babies certainly wasn't unheard of back then, but no-one could prove anything, even if they had tried.

All there was, was a bunch of fast, fading memories, circumstantial evidence, wild speculation, creeping visions, a whole lot of strange coincidence, and then some straight-up, utter nonsense, that I could never believe and in-fact, I never would. Coincidence? Karma? Or was it simply fucking fate? It certainly did make me wonder at times, as I've already said?

Anyway, I was eventually adopted by some people when I was three years old, who took me on another long journey and another six thousand miles away from where I actually was at the time, before they ended-up in a messy divorce, a short two years later. By then, I was five years old, being shipped off to different relatives for awhile, none of which, were actually my own flesh and blood of course, they in turn, would shift me on to others, time after time, town after town, and then finally, country after country.

I spent a week or two here and a month or two there, never really knowing where I was going to in the first place, or even who it was, that I would actually end-up with next and of course, that kept me travelling around for another five-years, with another forty-thousand-miles tucked underneath my belt, and for some reason, there were always motorcycles around, no matter where I went, or who I ended up with.

By the time I was eight years old, my head was spinning around so damn fast, that I really didn't know which way was up anymore, if I ever did to begin with?

And as far as schools went, I remember going to four of them in the same year but don't ask about my grades, because I was never around long enough to get any. But I sure could ride a motorcycle by then, and I knew how to keep it upright and in-between the lines.

My life had been pulled from pillar to post, never staying anywhere for more than a month or two at a time, and never with the same people neither.

In-fact, there was always someone different along the way and it was always somewhere that I had never been to before, and there were always way too many times when I'd wake up in the middle of a cold, dark night, screaming inside of my own head, just to find out that I was actually on my own again, wondering what in the hell would happen to me next?

A couple more years, a half-a-dozen more foster homes and who really knows how many sick, twisted, wannabe Dad slash, Mother types later; I ended-up on the streets, running from the Law and just about everything else. I didn't know where I was going, but I sure was going anyway and this time, I'd be the one to decide where that was, not them.

It forced me to grow-up quick and I grew-up pretty damn hard, right along with it. I also grew-up alone, no matter how many people were around me at any given moment in time, but most of all, I grew-up without a single thought in my head, about the way that things could've, would've, should've been, because I had never known that kind of life to begin with, and to be honest, by that moment in time, I really didn't care to know about it anyway. Everything beyond what I was doing was just a fantasy and I didn't have time for any of that shit…. Disconnect.

****

My next recollection, was suddenly waking-up alone again, cold, hungry, thirsty, and slightly disorientated, stuck in a small, damp room, that was completely void of any light, warmth, sound or feeling, crying out for my mother, who wasn't there. Again, all I had on was a diaper and some bandages that were wrapped-up tight around my head, eye, hand and arm, so I assume that it wasn't too long after my accident with the pan on the stove, but I couldn't be sure of that neither, because it might have been weeks or even a couple of months later? I was never a healthy child to begin with, born premature, with certain complications, including a hole in my heart and sub-standard lungs, but fortunately, I managed to grow out of most of those problems through the years, to a certain degree at least.

The room itself was completely bare, except for the baby crib that I was standing in and there was some sort of cot, or a single bed, that was lined up against the opposite wall, which once again, I could only assume that my mother had been using during the time that we had been staying there.

How long was that? I really have no idea; I just knew that it wasn't my usual place of sleeping, in-fact, I was quite sure that it was one of the many that I had already experienced, during my short existence.

The door of the room was in the centre of the inside wall, which was on his right side at the time, and it was closed just as tight as it could get, but I could still see a certain amount of light at the bottom of it, so I knew that it must have been daylight hours, or at least early enough to be awake, hopefully let out of my crib and then eventually fed, which was probably my main and ultimate concern at the time.

I've never been known for my patience though and back then it was probably less than your average child, so the more I cried out for my mother, the more agitated I became, knowing that the woman wasn't answering me in the first place and as you would imagine, my cries quickly turned into screams of anger, along with panic, confusion, hunger, thirst and then finally some sort of deep, primal rage, that quickly overcame me.

The next thing I knew is that I had managed to overturn the crib that I was in and drop myself to the floor of that darkened room, heading straight for the door of course, just as fast as my little feet could get me there.

Beyond the door, which to this day, I really have no idea of how I got it opened in the first place, was a long corridor with windows that stood side by side, stretching upwards from a wide windowsill to the ceiling, rapidly arching themselves at the top and stopping just short of the sill at the bottom.

They appeared to be spaced all the way along the outside wall, while the inside of the corridor was simply a long line of identical doors, spaced out in ten foot segments, just like the one that I had emerged from.

I remember that the doors were blue, the walls were an off white and the windows were crystal clear, clean and bright. I also remember that there was a square type of pattern that was laid-out on the floor, which was composed of half-dark and half-light tiles, while everything else around, seemed to be too damn clean, an immaculate setting, or at the very least, bright, quiet and almost spotless. Some sort of hospital I quickly thought at the time, or as I found out later, it was the children's home that I'd be adopted from.

Outside, the sun was shining, the skies were clear, bright blue and the grass was about as green as it could get and as I peered through one of the windows, I could see a group of people standing together, way off in the distance, along with several children that seemed to be running here, there and just about everywhere, each one playing with the others, laughing and having a good time.

Naturally, I climbed-up onto the windows ledge and started banging on the window with my free hand, trying to get their attention as best as I could, yelling out loud, inside my head of course, "Hey you guys, what about me? I'd like to come out and play as well." But no-one was listening, in-fact no-one was looking in my direction anyway and no-one could hear me, even if they had wanted to.

I don't know how long I stood there staring out that window, merely minutes I suppose, but it was long enough for me to see a fairly beautiful, young woman, with long, dark flowing hair and a slender petite figure, leading a prized looking animal through the crowd of children, heading towards the very spot that I was standing at.

I was excited that someone had noticed me after all and that they were on their way towards me. In-fact, I was quite sure that the woman was actually my birth-mother and she was leading a magnificent looking horse, for me to pet and maybe play with, at least that's what I thought at the time. She was probably my mothers sister, but I really don't know for sure?

Of course I didn't know it was a horse either, because I'd never seen a horse before, but as I stood there watching, I began to notice that an older man was waving his arms at the woman, yelling at her, while shaking his head at the same time, and then I watched as she, with a great deal of sadness in her eyes and her head held low, quickly turned around and led the horse away from me altogether.

My immediate reaction, was to start banging on the window again, yelling out as loud as I could, inside my head of course, "Come back, come back, please come back," crying and screaming out, with every breath I took, desperately watching as my mother disappeared into the distance, while at the same time, I could feel the life of me, being sucked out of my body faster than I had ever known before.

That one little moment, that single, defining and decisive moment in the life of a two year old child, simply tore the heart and soul right out of me, leaving me just as cold, empty and alone, as death itself.

I turned around after that, and practically ran back to that empty room, slamming the door behind me, as tightly as it had ever been before, and then of course the darkness that I had already known; immediately fell down around me again and I was quickly absorbed back into the emptiness of it all.

I never saw the woman after that, in-fact; I didn't see much of anything else for awhile neither and if I did, it was nothing that I cared to remember anyway.

That's what the emptiness does to a person. That's what the emptiness really is. It's a complete lack of everything, that's suddenly been turned into nothing and then nothing, is turned into emptiness, until the emptiness itself, is all that's left.

We've all had a little emptiness in our lives from time to time and I don't think it can be avoided, but this is where it started for me and I reckon it's as plain and simple as that.

****

14
Twisted steel

It was another long, hot and sticky, summer afternoon, when he suddenly found himself stuck out in the middle of nowhere, underneath a wide open, pale blue, West Texas sky, without a single cloud in sight and barely a breeze in the air.

Billy Lee Brixton had been standing there alone, for far too long at that point in time, looking up and down a long and empty stretch of desert highway, for what seemed to be hours and hours, waiting quite patiently for someone to come along and give him a ride.

It wasn't something that he was used to though and it certainly wasn't something that he had planned for, because he'd usually be flying down the road under his own steam so to speak, riding high on a hog, like a man on a mission, who was keeping it upright and in between the lines, just as fast as the road ahead would take him, but this time, well this time things had turned out a little different.

This time, things had gone to hell in a bucket, and he was standing in the middle of the flames. Who would've thought?

****

Now the back tire of the custom-made chopper that he'd been riding on for days and weeks by then, had suddenly frayed, popped and splintered, quickly going flat with a loud bang, which of course, effectively rendered his modern day horse, made from custom American made steel, lots of shiny chrome and totally tricked out paint, completely useless, leaving him, high and dry at the same time.

Oh well, that's just my luck these days, he quickly thought, as he stood there, stuck in the middle of nowhere, sweating like a fat pig at a rodeo that had been caged-up, waiting to be slaughtered and then cooked over an open fire.

He was utterly parched, chaffed and dry, patiently hoping for someone to come along and help him out. Someone that he knew would come his way, no matter what, someone that simply had to, eventually.

Patience had never been high on his list of virtues though and today wasn't going to be any different. The truth of the matter is that he was a long ways away from where he needed to be and now, he was starting to realize that he probably should have left a whole lot earlier.

He looked around at the empty span of desert that stretched out for literally miles in all directions. Of all the places that he could have broken down, this one was just about the worst one that he could think of.

There wasn't a tree in sight. There wasn't a bridge or a house or even a barn. All there was: was that bloody desert and there were literally too many miles of that.

Suddenly, he felt a strange, uneasy feeling, slowly creeping up from the pit of his stomach, as he stood there reeling from the heat of the day. It was a hundred degrees in the shade if not more, and a strange kind of wickedness had just swept across the middle of his back and then moved up and down both of his sides at a different rate of speed.

At the same time, a cold, damp tingle, slowly rippled itself all the way up his spine and then back down again, to a point somewhere near the base of it. There was also a knotted feeling, growing in the pit of his stomach and then suddenly, for no real reason at all, he just felt like throwing up, dry heaving for almost a minute or more, while he was standing there, waiting for someone to come along and get him the hell out of that place.

Afterwards, he needed a drink; and there was no doubt about that. Perhaps even a bite to eat as well, but there wasn't much hope of that neither, because he certainly hadn't planned for a picnic along the way, and then there was a sudden sense of a insane desperation, that completely overwhelmed him for a brief moment in time, which seemed to have a touch of déjà vu thrown in, just for good measure I suppose, or at least something that seemed to be a whole lot like it, because as he stood there looking around, he started feeling that he must have been down this road before at some point in time, and yet he knew that that wasn't possible, or was it?

"Where's a fucking ride when you need it the most?" he yelled out loud, with a natural but nervous irritation, trying to convince himself that this feeling was just plain stupid, while casually wiping the sweat away from his eyes and off of his forehead which was already dripping off the tip of his brow.

He watched slightly amused as a flock of birds flew out of the clutter of bushes that were gathered together on the other side of the road, just up from where he was standing. He carried on watching, as those same birds flew upwards, onwards and outwards, until they were completely out of sight. Then he turned around and tripped on a large rock that was laying there at the side of the road, twisting his ankle slightly at the same time. Yeah, that fucking hurt.

No-one had answered his question of course; after all, there was no one around to answer it. He was totally alone.

Now that was pretty stupid, he thought, as he stood there kicking out at one of the smaller stones that laid on the ground around him, looking back towards where he had just come from and then turning around again to look at where it was that he should be going to.

He knew eventually, that someone would come along, because they always did. He had never gotten himself into a jam that he couldn't get out of and this wasn't going to be the first one. It would take a little time that's all, just a little time.

That sun was directly over his head, beating down on him, like a giant heat lamp in one of those sleazy little saunas that you read about in girly magazines. It was brutal and it was beginning to affect the way that he was breathing. He was only able to manage short, shallow breaths at the moment, before the actual heat of the air started to irritate the inside of his lungs.

I swear it has to be a hundred degrees out here, maybe even more, he thought again, as he stood there dripping those precious little droplets of moisture onto the ground around him. Then he stared listlessly as a big ole desert rabbit, suddenly jumped up and darted across the road in front of him, running into the field and then quickly slipping itself into a deep, dark, hidden hole.

Now that's a pretty good idea, he thought again, as he looked around, but there was nowhere to go. There was nowhere for him to get any shade at all, he just had to stand there and wait, and then finally, he had to stand there and wait some more.

How long had it been now, an hour maybe two? The sun still hadn't moved. It was as though that infernal globe was stuck in the same damn spot, constantly shining down on him like some kind of gigantic torch, sitting high up in the sky, getting hotter and hotter all of time.

He had taken his jacket off, as soon as he stopped the bike, after blowing out the back tire. Then he took his shirt off a little while later and then finally, he took off his under shirt and tied it around his head.

His skin was already too damn hot; it was also turning red in the heat of the day and probably starting to blister, but he didn't have any choice in the matter, he just had to stand there and wait for some help to arrive.

It was a good job that he had brought some water with him; he thought as he reached into his saddlebags. Uh oh, where had he put it? Ah there it is, he thought again as he finally found it. It was only a little bottle really, maybe half a pint at the most, but it should be enough to get him through the mess he was in at the moment.

He took a few sips from the bottle before he realized that the water was about as warm as piss and probably even hotter than that, so he just swirled it around in his mouth and then he spat it back out towards a small lizard that he had noticed was sunning itself, along the side of the road, in the desert sand, close to his feet.

It didn't even move as his spit practically splashed it.

Never mind he thought again, as he placed the cap back on the bottle, then put the bottle back into deepest part of his saddle bags, right next to the hammerless .357 that he always carried. After all, you never know when some fool will try to rob you or something worse.

He usually carried it strapped to his side, but he had removed it as just quickly as he could when the tire blew out and he had to pull over. It was just too hot and too heavy, to be carrying it there in the heat.

He looked back down the highway from where he had just come from once again, but there was still nothing there, not a single car or truck in sight. He turned around and looked the other way, but it was just the same, nothing but empty space, with nothing moving, not a bird or a rabbit, or even a coyote.

It was right about then that he realized just how much he really hated those west Texas highways. They were without a doubt, the longest, loneliest roads in the world and as straight as an arrow for mile after mile. They're endless really, he thought, spanning across an entire nation, coast to coast, border to border, and connecting with other roads, from State to State. They cross over everything that gets in their way and every once in a while they'll go under something like a bridge, or a mountain or even a skyscraper or two.

There's at least one highway out west that actually goes through the centre of a tree, somewhere in Arizona or California? Which is pretty cool when you think about it?

Texas roads were always a great ride though, once you got away from the cities and towns. There was little traffic and even less cops, especially if you were used to being stuck inside a city like New York, Boston, Los Angeles or Chicago or any other concrete jungle that you can imagine for that matter and he knew them all, only too well.

There wasn't a city in the nation, that he hadn't been to at one time or another, from Fairbanks and Alert Alaska in the north, down to Key Lagos, in the south and all those points in between.

New York to L.A. was a consistent trip that he'd make, at least a couple of times a year and then there was Boston to Seattle and Vancouver BC to Toronto, which sometimes stretched on to Halifax, Nova Scotia or even St. Johns Newfoundland, depending on what time of year it was and how the weather turned out of course.

Getting stuck in a blizzard on a scoot wasn't a lot of fun, but it could be done easy enough, that's for sure, just not a real preference of his, more like a pain in the back side. Not to mention the cold.

He'd been through all of that before though and the cities that went along with it, and as far as he was concerned, you could keep every last one of them;

He preferred the open roads of the country, along with its forgotten highways every time, except for in a blizzard of course. That was the only time that a city was better than the country side.

You could crank up the throttle and catch the wind for hours in the country, if you wanted to and most of the time that was exactly what he wanted to do. He love to ride; in fact he lived to ride and when you really think about it, it's the next best thing to flying. It's quiet and peaceful, with only the sound of the wind rushing by your ears and the sun's rays on your back and of course that awesome purr of your engine running at about 7000 rpm's or maybe more.

It really is something special, scooting down the road like that, right up until you have to stop, that is. That's when you want to find a place to pull into that has some air-conditioning or a heater during the winter, along with good food and pleasant conversation of course, a place with comfortable furnishings and plenty of cold beers to wash away all of the dust and grime that you've accumulated at the back of your throat from being out there for hours on end in the first place. A great looking barkeep or a waitress with a huge smile, long legs and a healthy personality never hurts neither, and if she has a twin sister or even a friend that looks pretty much the same, you might just find yourself thinking about staying there for a little while longer than you should. You know what I'm saying. Life on the road can be pretty damn sweet at times, even for a biker.

****

Anyway, there he was on his way to El Paso, to put his super-charged, tricked-out, painted-up, iron horse, into a national bike show. He was hoping to take the "Twenty-five Thousand Dollar" first prize that was up for grabs.

It would help him to recoup some of the money that he had spent on building the damn thing to begin with and of course he could always use the cash for other things as well, because let's face it, he's never been a rich man by any means and money had always been pretty hard to come by, let alone trying to keep and like anyone else in this world that wasn't born with a silver spoon in their mouth, he could always find a good use for it. Who couldn't really? He just had to get there in time and win it.

Now, Sonny Barnett, who owned one of the largest Harley Davidson motorcycle shops in the world, which was located just outside of old El Paso, always put on a bike show at least once a year and quite often even twice.

This year he was bound and determined to take that prize money, if he could only get there in time that is, but somehow, at this particular moment, it didn't look as if he'd make it at all.

Where in the world is all of the traffic, especially when you really need them the most? He thought again. You'd think that at least one car, truck or even another motorcycle would have caught up with him by now. He can't be the only person heading towards the border. What about all of those people that live around here, don't they drive? By the way, what time is it? He thought as he looked down at his watch.

"Oh yeah, that's just fucking perfect" he said out loud, as he watched the second hand sitting there doing absolutely nothing? He quickly shook it a few times and then he shook it some more. It still didn't move and it looked like it wasn't ever going to move again. He was growing more and more impatient by then and his temper was starting to flare, right along with his temperature that was already too damn high.

"Ah to hell with this," he said out loud, as he took the watch off of his wrist and shook it some more. And yeah, that's just what I needed right now," he yelled out again, instinctively throwing the watch upwards and outwards, just as far as he could, into the empty desert span, that was spread out in front of him.

"Now I don't even know what time it is," he said again, talking to himself louder than he usually does. I don't know what time it is and I'm stuck in the middle of a damn desert, in the middle of the day with no-one else around. Damn it all, he thought, and then he realized what he'd just done?

He was starting to lose the plot. That watch had been a gift from a good friend of his, a brother from another mother type of friend. He couldn't just throw it away like that. It didn't matter whether it worked or not, he still needed to keep it, for the sake of their friendship, if nothing else.

He quickly walked towards the direction of where he felt the watch would be laying and started looking around for it. It had to be there somewhere? It couldn't have just disappeared like that, now could it?

He kept searching in expanding circles, growing frantic by the minute. He was becoming completely obsessed with finding it. In fact, it had become an all or nothing situation, a manic type of compulsion, consuming his every thought and desire.

He had to have the watch back, right now, no matter what it took and yet he didn't really know why? It wasn't like it was an expensive watch to begin with and he could always buy another one just like it, anywhere at any time really.

Anytime, except for right now that is and although it really was a gift from a good friend of his, he could always find another one to replace it and no-one in the world would be any wiser, except for him of course.

No-one would ever know the difference, especially his friend and he was pretty sure by then that he wouldn't really mind anyway, even if he did know about it. Hell, he'd just laugh about it and then tell him that it was just another cheap watch to begin with and hardly worth the effort. But somehow, for some insane reason, this had become more than just a principal to him now, it had become an all out obsession, a belief in the fact that he needed to find that watch no matter what it took, even if he had had to search for it for the rest of his life, he would, which at this point in time, and all of this heat, probably wouldn't be too damn long anyway; but regardless of that, he just had to find it and that was all there was to it, he had to get it back and he was sure that he would, eventually.

Then, as luck would have it, as he was still senselessly searching for it, getting further and further out in the field, he quickly turned his head around just in time to see a car that had slowed down by his bike that was parked-up alongside of the road. The only car that he had seen for literally hours, the only car that was on the road in either direction, the only car that could have actually stopped and helped him out of the mess that he was in, and he had turned his head around just in the nick of time to watch it simply speed up and drive away.

"No, no, no," he said, running towards the highway as fast as he could go, but it was pointless by then, the car was already gone. It was clean out of sight by the time he got back to the bike.

"Damn it", he said out loud again and again, sweating, panting and puffing, almost completely out of breath, how stupid can a guy get? That friggin watch has got to be some sort of a jinx."

Then, right out of the blue, he just happened to glance down at the side of the road where he was standing and he saw something laying there, something that was shining back at him, almost smiling at him, like that proverbial grin on the Cheshire cat, in the movie of Alice in Wonderland.

He walked straight over to it and picked it up. Would you believe it, it was his watch.

"Whoa, that's way too fucking weird; he thought, as he quickly bent over to get it. He could have sworn that he had chucked this thing way out in the desert. So, how in the hell did it get back here?"

He looked up at the sun again. It still hadn't moved, although it seemed like it had grown double its size. In fact, he was sure that it was larger than he had ever seen it before, but he didn't know if that was really the case or not, because his head was spinning around so fast by then and he was feeling sick to his stomach again. He needed to sit down for a while because he was seriously beginning to overheat.

If only the sun would hurry up and make its way across the sky, or perhaps a few clouds could form and the wind could pick up a little, then maybe he could sit down in the shade of his bike for a while and cool off, but the sun wasn't moving. It just stayed there, hovering overhead and the more he looked at it, the dizzier he got.

He sat down on the side of the road for a quick rest. His head was spinning pretty fast by then and even with his shades on, the light was becoming unbearable. It was hurting more than just his eyes so he laid back for a few minutes, closing them tight, pulling the t-shirt down over them, and then enjoying the much needed rest, especially from his recent run around the field.

He was exhausted from the heat as it was, so he's really not sure how long he stayed like that. It could have been a minute or two, or maybe even five or ten, but it wasn't long until he suddenly opened up his eyes again and he was scrambling to get back on his feet.

Something had just stung him and then there was another one and another one. Ahhh shit he screamed, feeling the pain and burning sensations that were beginning to work their way all over his body as he jumped to his feet, stamping on the earth and gravel at the same time, circling around himself again and again, stamping more and more, harder and harder.

He must have looked like a half crazed, homeless person, or a Red Indian, doing a bloody rain dance or something even stranger, but then he finally realized what was going on. The road was crawling with red ants and a few of them had decided to check out his legs for lunch.

He practically ripped his trousers off in one sheer swoop, standing there all but buck-naked, except for the riders on his feet, his socks of course and the T-shirt around his head, carefully inspecting them all for anymore of those pesky little assassins that were out to do him in.

"Great!" he yelled at the top of his lungs, just frickin great, what else could possibly go wrong. Damn it all, this is definitely not what I needed now, especially when I'm stuck out in the middle of nowhere.

He quickly put his trousers back on as soon as the inspection was over, but he knew that he only had about twenty-six minutes left to actually get to a hospital and get a shot of adrenaline and anti-histamine before he started to keel over.

You see, he's highly allergic to bug bites, wasps, bees, spiders and especially ants. He's been that way all his life, ever since he was kid, so he knew that he was pretty screwed up now, that's for sure.

What he needed was some pure antihistamines, along with a shot of adrenaline and a whole lot of water as well, but of course, he didn't have anything like that with him, although you'd think that he would have, knowing what would happen if he ever did get stung, but to be honest, it was probably the last thing on his mind when he left the hotel that morning. It was just too nice of a day and all he was thinking about, was getting to the bike show. He never dreamt that he'd be stuck out on the damn highway for any reason, let alone because of a flat tire.

Anyway, that's what he needed, sure enough, it was that or maybe some kind of anti-venom injection straight into his veins, if there was such a thing?

He looked back down the road again. Still not a car in sight and now, time, was definitely running out.

What the hell am I going to do now, he thought? I only have one choice really, I have to jump back on the bike and hobble it down the road, flat tire or not. I have to try. So, he stood there thinking about it for a minute or two.

The wheel on the rear of his motorcycle had cost him well over three thousand dollars to put together. It was specifically made as wide as he could get it at the time and the rim was made out of pure cast aluminium. Three thousand dollars was a lot of money back then, but it was either that, or else take a chance on losing his life by doing nothing at all. Suddenly, three thousand dollars seemed pretty cheap considering the alternative. So he jumped up on the bike, kicked the stand and pushed the button, wouldn't you know, nothing happened? What the hell, he thought to himself again, what's going on now? He tried the starter again and again, but still nothing happened. Everything was dead, not even the tail light was working.

"Oh man, he said out loud, it just doesn't get any better than this. Now I've got a dead battery and I'm stuck out in the middle of a fucking desert, in the middle of the day and it just happens to be in the middle of the bloody week as well. Who would have thought?"

He was fuming. He could also feel his heart picking up its beat, racing towards that final pump, the very last one that he would ever have, if he didn't get help fast.

His heart usually ran steady at about sixty-seven beats a minute or so, but it was probably up to a hundred and ten by then and it wasn't going to slow down any time soon. There had been a few other times in his life when he had come close to dying from a bug bite. One time in particular, was when he was bitten by a spider on his lower left leg in the middle of the night.

When he woke up, apart from the searing pain that it caused and the black hole that it created, he also watched as a thin red line, slowly travelled up his leg, past his groin, on to his lower stomach, and from there it went all the way up his stomach towards his heart. Fortunately, he got to the hospital just in time with that one, but he was kept on an I.V. drip, for literally weeks afterwards. There was no chance of that happening now though, even if someone had stopped in time to help.

So, you have to know that he really figured that he was dying out there and there wasn't any doubt about it in his mind. A bad situation had just gone to the worst situation that he could have possibly got himself into, no matter what and all in matter of minutes really and there was simply nothing that he could do about it.

****

Now most people would have considered getting their pistol out of their saddle bags and then putting it up to their own head at that point in time, which was what he was contemplating, he'd have to admit that, because dying from anaphylactic shock, or any other kind of blood poisoning in the middle of a desert, middle of the day or not, certainly isn't the best, or even the easiest way to go.

So, he thought about it all right, he thought about it real hard, but he wasn't going to be beaten yet. He wasn't going to be the victim here if he could help it.

He wasn't going to be some sort of statistic that someone else finds out about, days or even weeks later, that's for sure.

"That fucking devil could go straight back to hell" he yelled out as loud as he could.

You see, if the truth was known, he had always been a stubborn son of a bitch when he wanted to be, and apart from that, he just figured that no matter what, it wasn't his time to die and it was as plain and as simple as that.

Then completely out of the blue, standing in the middle of nowhere, half way into nothing, he suddenly heard a voice, just as clear, as clear could be.

"Is that a fact? The old man said, standing there, right next to him and his motorcycle. What makes you think anything like that could be your choice to begin with Billy?"

"What in the hell," he said, "Who are you and where on God's green earth did you come from?" He looked up and down the road real quick for the old man's car, but he couldn't see it anywhere.

"Exactly," the old man said, "Now answer my question."

"What? What question are you on about?" Billy said, still searching for the old man's car, but it just wasn't there, in-fact there was nothing to be seen at all, not even an old donkey or a tired assed mule like they had in the movies that those old prospectors used to ride away on, way back when.

"There ain't no car here Billy, the old man said, so just answer my question or it'll be the last one that I ask you."

"Ok, he said, what question was that? I don't remember you asking me any questions in the first place?

"I said the old man spoke firmly once again, what makes you think, that it could be your choice to begin with?"

"I still don't get it, he said, "How could you even begin to know what I was thinking about and how in the hell do you know my name?"

"Just answer the question Billy." The old man said sternly, looking at him with a slight smile on his face, but there was a distinct chill in his eyes.

They were cold, dark and piercing, as well as the weirdest looking blue that anyone has ever seen, in one eye only, and the darkest green in the other. You certainly didn't trust him, whoever he was.

"All right, all right, Billy said, it's my life and I'll end it when I feel like it, or when it's my slated time, and that won't be for the devil to decide or anyone else for that matter, it'll be my own decision and mine alone.

"All right then," the old man said, "What makes you think that it's not your slated time right now?"

"I'm way too young to die," he said, with a smile on his face and a fire burning in his own piercing blue/green eyes.

"Younger people than you have died Billy, the old man said; you know that, it happens all the time."

"Well then, I'm just too tough," he said again, clenching his fists, preparing himself for whatever was about to come his way, but nothing did.

The old man just stood there with an even bigger grin on his face, as though he was really enjoying the moment.

"A lot tougher men than you have died Billy," the old man said, smiling back at him, you know that, as well as I do. You ain't that tough now are you?"

"Okay, okay, he quickly said, the truth is that I'm too damn stubborn to die and I never give up, never have, and never will."

"Yeah and I guess you're not too smart right now, are you Billy boy, especially by putting yourself out in the middle of the desert like this. Shame on you and shame on you again for tempting an old man like me," he said, laughing out loud.

Billy was getting pretty irritated with this old fool and his stupid assed sense of humour by then, so he finally said to him, "Look old man, just piss off, I don't know who you think you are, but I'm sure that I don't owe you anything. I don't need you hanging around here messing with my head like this and I certainly don't want you here that's for sure and I'm pretty sure that I'm not going anywhere with you, if that's what you have in mind, so go on now, piss off and leave me alone."

"Actually, I think you really do need me Billy, the old man said reaching out to touch his chest. Your heart is racing faster than you can count, just like a raging bull and if you don't slow it down soon, it'll pop just like that back tire of yours did, back down there on the highway, and then I'm afraid you'll be mine forever with no hope in hell, he said again, laughing almost hysterically.

"Do you have a shot of something in your pocket old man? Because that's just what I need to slow this ole ticker down, that and some really good fucking luck for a change," he said, barely catching his breath.

His heart was pounding so hard now that the sweat was rolling off the top of his forehead down into his eyes and then continuing down to the tip of his nose, before it dripped off, onto the ground.

"Well I'd like to help you out if I could Billy, I really would indeed, the old man said, but as you can see, I'm not actually here, not in the physical sense of the word anyway, if you know what I mean? However, I reckon that if you walk on out to that cactus way over yonder, you could possibly jab one of its quills into your chest and that just might help you out for a little while. In fact, it would probably help you out quite a bit, if you were to think about. You never know, it might just be what the doctor ordered."

"Yeah right," he said to him again, like I'm really going to fall for that one yeah?"

He looked around and the old man was gone. He had vanished into thin air and now he figured that he really was losing it, in fact he was definitely dying for sure.

He had just been talking to some fictitious entity, in the middle of the desert, arguing with him about some cactus plant that he could barely see, not to mention the fact that it was way off in the distance and it would take a lot of time and effort to get to. So yeah, he felt that it wouldn't be too long now, because even if a ride did come by right now, at this moment, it wouldn't get him to the hospital on time.

He may as well have just put that bullet into the side of his head, just as he figured that he would have to do all the way along anyway.

He looked at the chopper that was sitting there as he got off of it again. It had cost him over three year's salary to finally put it all together. It was beautiful, it was long, low and mean looking, with that special paint, chrome and a back tire that was never meant to fail, but it certainly wasn't worth any of the effort or the blood, sweat and tears that I had lost over it now. It may as well have been just another piece of twisted steel sitting there at the side of the road, because that's what it was starting to look like now, to him anyway.

It was probably just the heat of the day, he quickly thought, that and the bug bites, but he looked up at the sun again and saw that it still hadn't moved. What the hell is going on with that? Is it ever going to get across that damn sky? Shit, he thought again as he felt a painful jolt, making its way up through his chest, his heart was definitely racing even more now, boom, boom, boom, boom, and boom.

"Maybe this cactus thing really is a good idea," he quickly thought again, after all, I certainly didn't have anything to lose, because if I stand there much longer, I'll die anyway.

"To hell with it," he said out loud, as he headed back out into that desert field.

It never occurred to him that if he actually dropped dead out there, they might never find his body, because the animals would have fed on it long before they even thought to look. Still what choice did he really have?

Now, it took him at least ten minutes to get to that plant or so it seemed at the time because it was a lot further away than what he thought. His legs were all swelled up and his lips were chapped and dry, hell they were even cracking by the time he finally got there. A trickle of blood was slowly oozing out of his left nostril and his head was pounding like a jack hammer. He was so dizzy that when he finally got to that plant, he just fell down to his knees at the foot of it.

Ahhh, another sharp pain ran across his chest and then upwards into his head. Ahhh, there it was again, this time it knocked him all the way to the ground. This is it, he quickly thought, as he struggled to keep himself from passing out. I'll be seeing that old man again real soon I guess? Then he swore that he heard him laughing at him again, as he suddenly appeared out of nowhere.

"I thought you told me you weren't a quitter, the old man said, smiling down at him. I thought you said that it wasn't your time to go, that you were too damn young to die and way too tough. You must have been talking about someone else then, I guess, because that person certainly doesn't look like you now, does he?"

"You again," Billy said, coughing his lungs out after the words that he practically spat out to begin with, you just can't wait until I finally kick it, can you old man?

What's your problem anyway? I told you that I ain't ready to die yet and I ain't, so go fly yourself a kite, upside down and sideways, all on your own down there in Hades for all I care, you old Devil, because you're just wasting your time up here with me, that's for damn sure."

"I don't know about that Billy Boy" the old man said, just look at those buzzards circling around; they always know where to get a good meal, don't they?"

"Yeah, well it ain't going to be me old man, not today anyway, he said, pulling himself over to the cactus; I'll stick two or three of these things inside of me, if it'll help." Then he reached up and broke off a hand full of quills.

"You better hurry now Billy, the old man said, because time just marches on and it sure ain't waiting for no one now, let alone you."

He took the quills and stabbed himself in the chest with them, they were long and thin, but they were full of cactus juice and they hurt like hell when he did it. It was even worse than the bloody bug bites to begin with, and he was sure that he heard that old man screeching out hysterically when he did it again and again. He had to be sure that he had put enough of that shit into his system to either counteract the bug bites or just kill him outright, didn't he? And then he heard the old man say,

"I'll see you later Billy Boy, have yourself a good rest now you hear, because you're definitely going to need it when all is said and done."

He finally dropped back down to the ground while his head spun around several more times and then simply passed out from all the pain that was searing through his body.

When he woke up, he didn't know how long he had laid there, but the buzzards had come swooping down on him in his dreams; they pecked around for a bit, trying to get at his eyeballs and all the other shit that was caked-up inside of his nostrils, but they finally left him alone when they realised that he wasn't quite dead yet. He wasn't going to be a meal for them today, they thought, perhaps they'd come back tomorrow or maybe they'd leave him to cook in the desert sun, for another day or two first.

When he finally opened up his eyes again, the first thing he saw was that damned fire ball in the sky. It still hadn't moved, not anywhere, in-fact, not at all and it was just as big and as hot and just as bloody powerful, as it had been all day long.

"This is way too frigging much," he thought, looking up at it again, it was still directly over his head, beating down on him, like a giant heat lamp in a sauna.

He struggled to get to his feet again, feeling pretty damn weak and feeble at first. He certainly wasn't used to feeling that way, that's for sure. Ordinarily he was as strong as an ox and yeah, he was probably just as dumb at times. Years of riding had put a lot of muscle in all the right places, and it had kept the fat off as well. Besides that, he was still a young man really, usually healthy as a horse as they say. He was also still dizzy though, but he noticed that his head wasn't pounding nearly as hard now as it was before; in-fact, it was barely pounding at all.

Damn, he thought again, that old man was right on the money, those cactus quills have done some sort of magic on me. He felt all over his legs. They were still pretty puffy, red and sore, especially around the bite marks, but the swelling was going down and they didn't sting half as much as they had before. That's good he thought again, because it was time to get back to his bike.

He got up, onto his feet, steadied himself for a moment and then took a good, long, look around. He didn't like what he saw. "Damn it all to hell again", he said, which way is it? I can't even see the road from here, damn it, damn it, and then damn it some more." Then he heard that old man's laughter again, as he quickly turned around to face him.

"You'll still be mine by the time this day is over Billy, the old man said with a chuckle, unless you're smarter than you look right now. I guess those Army days didn't teach you much of anything, did they?" The old man just kept on talking without waiting for an answer. "Special Forces, wasn't it? Airborne Rangers, Forward Recon and all of that hard ass shit that you went through, back in the day, yeah, you can shoot a gun for fun Billy Boy, and you're even better when people are shooting back, but you can't tell which way is up most of the time, especially these days, now can you?"

"Get back down to hell old man, he said; don't you know they're called weapons in the Army? Guns are for fun or maybe for the girly girls and I ain't ever been one of those, so talk about me not knowing anything?"

"Now, now, be nice to me Billy Boy, because what I really know is that you can't see the road from here and I also know that you only have four ways that you could go and three of them will lead you straight back to me no matter what. The fourth will get you back to the road and back to your pretty little motorcycle eventually, but I'll bet you don't take that one, so what do you think about those odds Billy? Do they scare you?" The old man said, laughing right out loud.

"I'd say that those odds, as you call em, are in my favour, you old devil, he said, smiling as he said it, don't you know that us Army brats have always been rated as the under dogs anyway."

"Yeah, that's right Billy, poor little ole you, the old man said, let me see if I have a hanky to wipe away those tears you're about to cry, Hmm, here's one right now, just blowing in the wind."

He turned around just in time to see a small piece of blue cloth blow right on by him. He thought for a moment about the situation that he was in and how he might be able to turn it around to his advantage, if he only used his head that is.

"I'll tell you what old man, he said, If I can't walk out of here and find my bike, I'll be happy to go with you, to where ever it is that you want me to go to, without a fuss or even an argument, but if I can walk out of here and I do find my bike, then I want you to put it back together for me, back into its original shape, so that I can get on it and get the hell out of this God forsaken desert, away from that screwed up sun that seems like its stuck out there in the middle of the sky and even further away from you old man. How does that sound to you?"

"Are you trying to make a deal with me Billy Boy? Don't you know that I could just wait for you to completely fry yourself out here? Don't you know that I could just walk away from all of this in a heartbeat and wait my time, the old man said; sooner or later you'll be with me anyway. What does it matter when or where, I've got all the time in the world and then some."

"What's the matter old man, Billy said, aren't those odds good enough for you? We're talking a Seventy five percent chance that you'll win anyway, what do you say old man, take the bet and prove to me, who it is that you think you really are, otherwise I'll just say that you're full of shit; you've got no power over me and you never will have. You're just a figment of my fucked-up imagination right now and that's all there is to that."

The old man just stood there for a few moments, looking at him and smiling as he always seemed to do. You could see that he was thinking about it and Billy knew that whatever he had on his mind probably wouldn't be too good for him anyway, but then the old man said.

"You put that hanky over your eyes Billy and I'll take that bet," just as the blue cloth flew around again and back into Billy's face.

"Put it over your eyes and spin yourself around ten times. It'll be a bet then, fair and square."

"Yeah right, Billy said, fair bet my ass. If you throw in a hanky to blindfold me, then, I want you to throw in some cash as well, in-fact I want you to fill up my saddle bags with it and I want nothing less than One hundred dollar bills, and just as many as those bags will carry."

The old man laughed out loud, cackling again as he had before.

"You know that you can't win in this situation Billy, he said, no one ever beats the Devil, but all right then, if you win. One Hundred dollar bills it is." He spat in his hand and held it out for Billy to shake but of course that didn't happen, it was gone when he reached for it and so was the old man, but a bet was a bet regardless and he was determined to win this one hands down.

He looked around for a moment noting where the cactus was, and then he put the cloth over his eyes and tied it tight. He spun himself around ten times just like he had been asked to do and then he fell to the ground.

When he got back up, he started walking with his arms stretched out wide, after a few steps he turned and walked a few more and then he turned again, finally after another turn he ran into the cactus bush.

He quickly felt around it and found what he was looking for, that moist bleeding scar, where he had pulled the quills out of its side earlier on. Then, he completely turned himself around again and walked straight on out of there just as fast as his feet could carry him. It took him about fifteen minutes to finally hit the gravel on the side of the road and let me tell you, he was more than just a little happy about that. He was ecstatic.

The old man knew that he had lost his bet. He wasn't smiling anymore as he watched him finally reach the edge of the road. He could have told Billy to keep the cloth on right up until he found his bike, but for some strange reason he didn't. He was only playing with him this time around and Billy really hoped that there wouldn't be another time, especially anytime soon.

"Next time I'll have you Billy and trust me there will be a next time for sure" the old man said with a growl, as he quickly disappeared again.

"Next Time" echoed through the air, lingering for the rest of the few moments that it took Billy to remove his blindfold. He took it off, blinked a few times and then looked up the road towards where his bike was sitting, with its perfect back tire and its bulging saddlebags and then he just started laughing. He practically ran the rest of the way and then he jumped on it and started it up with a push of the button.

Finally, he looked back out across the desert from where he had just been. He could barely see the cactus that was almost shining in the distance; it was the only thing that looked like a piece of twisted steel in that hot desert sun now.

He looked up at the sky, flipped his middle finger at that ball of fire, put his shirt and jacket back on and then he slowly squeezed the clutch, kicked it into gear and roared off like a man on a mission.

A storm was approaching; and he could smell the rain in the air. He could also feel it on his breath. He still had a long ways to go, but at least the air that he was breathing now, was quickly cooling off and wouldn't you know it, the bloody traffic had finally started to pick up again, who would've thought?

He managed to tuck himself up behind an old tractor-trailer as it passed him by and he cruised there for awhile before the rain finally hit. The trailer kept most of the rain off of him for awhile as he headed down the road behind it and when it finally pulled into a truck stop, about an hour or so further west of where he had already been, he could see that there was a pretty good looking woman truck driver sitting behind the steering wheel, so he went ahead and parked up as well.

Never being shy about the fairer sex, he introduced himself as quickly as he could and eventually bought her a cup of coffee and some lunch, while sharing her table and some light conversation of course, finally telling her, his entire ordeal about being stuck out in the desert, as they sat there eating.

He probably shouldn't have done that, but the woman didn't really seem to mind, in-fact, as luck would have it, she was on her way to El Paso as well, with a little time on her hands and of course, he had a lot of that himself now, with money to burn and nowhere in particular to be.

****

15
Shamaiya

There's a lot of things about El Paso, that people really loved back in the day, perhaps even more than the weather, which was always hot, clear, and dry, and if you rode a motorcycle, that's exactly what you wanted, clear blue skies, long, hot, lazy roads, and the ability to catch the wind, for literally hours at a time. But the best thing about El Paso was the fact that it's one of the gateways to Mexico.

Juarez to be more specific, just across the street really, which for Billy and so many others that he had known along the way, was the one thing that they had all cherished the most, simply because you could buy things south of the border, a whole lot cheaper than you could buy them anywhere else, unless of course, you jumped on a plane, and went to the Far East, like Thailand or Singapore.

What was even better than that though, was the fact that you could get things across the border, that might be considered illegal, or even outlawed in the U.S at the time, but not necessarily illegal in Juarez or anywhere else in Mexico for that matter, and it was always easy enough, just to pop across the border for a day, or two, get what you wanted, and then pop on back again, just as quickly as you liked, and if you knew what you wanted to begin with and where to get it, it didn't take much time at all, but it's definitely not that simple now, and I suppose, that if the powers that be, actually get their way, it'll be practically impossible.

****

These days, it's just a bloody hassle right from the get go, no matter which border it actually is, and you can almost guarantee, that it'll take you hours to get through customs, whether you're coming or going, and believe me, when I say that the boys in Texas, definitely don't want you bringing things back with you, anymore.

No, no, that's just un-American, there's no patriotism in that after all, and way down in El Paso, Texas, you can bet that they are definitely into their patriotism, big time. They even have a saying down there that basically goes like this, "If it ain't Texas, then it ain't shit, and if it ain't shit, then it ain't worth nothing, nothing at all."

You can ask any of the good ole boys that live around there, and they'll all tell you the same. Texans are a pretty proud lot when it comes to that, after all Texas, is the biggest little country, in the whole of the US of A, and that's just the way they think about it. To them, it's a country not a state.

If you even look like you might have something that you shouldn't have, you're going get hassled, one way or another, and bikers always look that way, at least to them, that is. The border patrol, the customs agents, the TSA, the local yokels and of course, the good ole boys that run everything down there anyway. The list just goes on and on and everybody wants their piece of the pie, so to speak, they always have. It's a shame really, because it used to be a pretty good way of making some extra cash, for those that would actually take the time and the risk, but nowadays, that risk is pretty damn high, and most people can't be bothered with it anymore. Besides that, it's pretty much run by the Mexican Mafia, and some of their lackeys, on both sides of the law, and on both sides of the border, and they'll be the first to turn over an outsider to the law, especially a biker, for good measure, of course. But, never mind, times change, people change, and the law, well everyone knows that the "Law" is always changing.

Motorcycle clubs; get their money from variety of different revenues, as we all know. Most of their members are simply hard working, middle class types, that are more than happy to pay their dues once or twice a month, for the chance to be part of something bigger, than what they are alone, but the club is a business run by its members, from a President at the top, down to its soldiers, wannabees, and hanger-ons, at the bottom.

At least that's the way it used to be, but nowadays, clubs have a couple of dozen board members and trustees as well, along with other officers of the so-called corporation. OG's (old gangsters), bosses and associates, and of course way too many investors that probably don't even ride a motorcycle to begin with, let alone put on a leather jacket, and yet they still call the shots, whether you know it or not and they still want their dues. Money talks, bullshit walks and it's about as simple as that.

Clubs have grown into Corporations, and those Corporations simply absorb other Corporations. It's the way of the jungle, but in this case, it's a concrete jungle that we're talking about here and it's slowly dying a hideous death.

Combine all of that with new laws that are being passed every other week, along with the cost of business in the first place, like taxes, license fees and insurance money, and it makes you wonder why anyone would want to be a biker in the first place.

Still, if they're smart enough, they stay ahead of the law, and invest what little they have into legal venues, like dance and fitness clubs, or bars, restaurants and road houses, security companies, strip joints, and of course anything that deals with motorcycles and motorcycle parts, amongst a list of other things.

Any business that makes money is an opportunity for a motorcycle club, whether they own a piece of it or not, doesn't even matter in the grande scheme of things.

Having the largest motorcycle shop in the world aint a bad idea neither, but bike clubs are a whole lot bigger than that, they always were, and they're always hungry for more.

Now, a lot of clubs don't care about the law, and they go about their business, trying to break it, every chance they get. To them, it's just a game really; after all, laws change all the time. What was legal yesterday, won't be legal tomorrow, and most bikers know that, so they get in and take what they can, while they can, before the law finally catches up to them.

When that happens, a few bikers get arrested and the club spends a little money on lawyer's fees, bail bonds and care packages etc, without even skipping a beat in the real world. Some of its members may even do a little prison time for whatever, whenever and then, when they finally get out, they usually have one hell of story to tell, an extra tag on their jacket and an even a better party to go to, right before they start the same old game all over again. Of course, some of its members never do get out, for whatever reasons, but they know the stakes and they're all used to working the odds and some of them will even get rich doing it along the way, or they'll die trying.

You might say that, that's why they're called "Outlaws" to begin with, even though most of the clubs are owned, operated and registered, as legal businesses in every state, province, and country around the world that you can find them in.

They pay their taxes, workman's comp, business insurance and any other dues, just the same way as anyone else that's in business and yet they're labelled as "Outlaw" bike clubs and their members are commonly known as "outlaw bikers."

Unless you're down under of course, then they're called Bikies, for whatever reasons? Still 1%ers, are one percenters, whether they're truly outlaws or not.

****

What people don't really know is just how many bike clubs there are in today's society, or just how many members each club has. Another thing that people don't know, is who those members really are, because they're not all gypsies, tramps and thieves, as the law, the news or the government, tries to make you believe and they don't all wear rockers on their backs, or even a leather jacket for that matter.

Some of those bikers are actually doctors, lawyers, and judges, believe it or not and there are far too many cops and ex-cops, that are active patch-holding members of every so-called, outlaw motorcycle association out there.

Firemen, paramedics, soldiers and even the odd banker or two, are high on the list as well, and you probably know some of the millionaires and billionaires that ride with a patch on their back, as well as certain politicians, actors and musicians, that call themselves bikers.

All of those people that are well known to be full time patch-holders in the world of entertainment, high-finance and government, are at the very least, part time members of many of the world's most renowned motorcycle clubs, that everyone knows about today.

Almost anyone that has ever had an interest in motorcycles, can name the most famous bikers in the world, and everyone knows the name of the club that runs in their own neighbourhoods, but for every club that gets a mention, there are literally thousands, that most people will never even know about and every one of those, usually has at least fifty to a hundred members, if not more.

After all, strength is in the numbers. So the bigger you are, the badder you are and the hungrier you'll get.

These numbers are pretty staggering when you think about it, with well over five million patch-holding bikers, in the United States alone, not to mention Canada, Mexico and the rest of the world.

Add all of that with the joy rider clubs, solo riders, backwoods, cross country, and serious road racers and you will double or even triple that amount.

These people live and breathe motorcycles, every single day of their lives and they have friends and family that do exactly the same thing. Think about that for a moment.

Think about all of that revenue; think about all of that insurance money that keeps going up and up, hell, just think about all of those motorcycles and the cost of buying a new one in today's economy.

One percent of the world's population equals out to over Eight-hundred-million bikers worldwide, which may not be quite as big as China's army, which is said to be over a billion people strong, but it is pretty big none the less and it's growing all the time. Who knows, maybe China's army is full of bikers as well?

Imagine if all of those bikers got together to change the world into a better place. Imagine if every club member, joined forces with every other club member out there, and they all became members of one large, single, super club? Think about all the things that they could do for the world around them; think about what they could accomplish? What they could actually own and control?

A united society of motorcycle enthusiasts, at least Eight-hundred million strong, called the "S.M.E," or the Society of Motorcycle Enthusiasts.

****

Now, we're definitely not talking about going down the same routes that two or three largest motorcycle clubs in the world, have gone down before. Nor are we talking about some sleazy, low-life, gang-banger, ball-breaker type of scenario, which would only be in it for the anarchy and the money of course, and to hell with the little guys and all the rest of those that just want to ride around occasionally and rightly deserve to be able to do that as well. After all, money is only good for what it is, and it takes a lot more than money to heal the world from all of its problems, that's for sure.

What it really takes is a dream, a dream big enough to turn it all into a reality and a vision strong enough to get all of those bikers in the world together, at the same time, for exactly the same reasons. Think about that for a moment, it might be a dream, but it's a dream that many bikers would have liked to have seen come true at one point in time, especially when the world was still a younger place and the whole concept of motorcycles was fairly new.

Billy wasn't alone in those thoughts though; there were a lot of others, dreaming the same dream as well. He just happened to be an offspring of the one that came up with the name to begin with, the "S.M.E. ™"

Maybe it never happened, maybe there were always way too many barriers to overcome and far too many disputes to settle, and the real bottom line was, the fact that there was way too much greed and corruption on both sides of the law, and especially in the ones that started up all of those little clubs to begin with.

Maybe they could never get it together, because they were being torn apart every chance they got and eventually, they all just started fighting each other, first, in their own inner cities and counties and then moving on to complete provinces or States, until finally, they were at it all over the world, after all, every single club out there wants to be the biggest, the baddest and the ugliest club on the planet, or at least, in their own territories.

They became no different than some of the punk-assed, street gangs that ran amuck right along with them or even the ones that were there years before them.

Honour, Integrity, loyalty and trust as well as any kind of brotherhood, were words that every biker had tattooed in their minds, and on their bodies, at one time or another, but now, they're just signs of the past, "Old School shit" is what most of the younger ones say, and it's all down to greed when you think about it, simply because enough is never enough.

It didn't used be that way when he was younger; you could always trust your brothers back then and they always had your back no matter what, even if it meant going to prison or facing certain death.

You knew that you were a part of something that was so big, so special and so unique, that it could never be broken and it would never die. But as usual, things change, just as they always have and they always will.

Billy saw it coming though. He had a knack for that sort of thing, especially, back then. Maybe that's why he finally stopped being a patch-holder and went back out on his own to begin with. He could be anywhere he needed to be, when it was necessary and then he could be on his way again, and he wouldn't have to answer to anyone.

He didn't have to worry about who said what, when or where and he didn't have to stick around for the politics or answer any club members. He just did what he needed to do, no matter what that meant. Get in and get out as quickly as he could, because that's what he was known for anyway, and that's what he had always been good at doing.

He learned his skills in the army as a "Reconnaissance Specialist", spending time getting in and out of enemy territory, doing black ops, TDY's, skirmishes, and sorties etc. without being noticed, and without getting caught, so it was the perfect road to travel down with the S.M.E. as well, but then again, maybe that's not really the case; maybe there is no S.M.E at all. I'll just leave you with that thought for the moment and we'll get on with the story.

****

Five days later, that woman truck driver that Billy had hooked-up with after his last time out in the desert, was up with the sun and gone with the wind so to speak, just as the song says, and so was his money.

He never did get to the bike show; instead he wasted himself, and most of his time, on a good looking, female truck driver, along with lots of party favours and a fancy hotel room that he'll never see again. Yeah, it'd been fun for sure, she was beauty for her age and she certainly knew how to party. She was damn good at it as well, but the fun never lasts that long, and when reality sets in, it can bite you pretty hard at the best of times. So, he woke up alone, wondering why in the hell he was still inside that fancy hotel room to begin with, where was the woman that he had been with the nights before, and more to the point, where was all his money?

Typical luck he thought, just another stupid plan that didn't quite work out right. You'd think a guy like him, would have known better than to trust a woman with anything, but he had always been a sucker for a pretty face and that certainly hadn't changed much over the years, regardless of what they'd put him through. They may have more lines under their eyes these days, a softer body and a few extra pounds that they probably shouldn't have, but he was still a sucker for em, just the same. He couldn't help that. He loved his women, he always had, and always would and I guess, it really is, just as simple as that.

At least he had his wits about him to begin with. He had put the bike in the shop straight away and it was checked out in no time, and then he had gone to the bank, as soon as he could get there.

He walked in with his saddle bags strung over his shoulder and then he dropped forty-grand on the counter in a heartbeat.

The staff looked at him, as if he had robbed another bank somewhere, with their eyes almost popping out of their sockets, and their jaws hanging wide open, but he stood his ground, counting the money for them, dressed in his tattered jeans, tee-shirt and black leather jacket. He didn't care what they thought? But he swears that they didn't know what to do with him at first. Whether to call the cops or not?

It all turned out fine by the end though and he was certainly smiling a lot when he got the receipt and walked back out the same door that he came in through.

That old man had done him well, there was actually fifty grand, inside his saddle bags when he left the desert that day, fifty grand, was more than a couple of years' salary for most people back then, and ten grand more than he would've got, if he had won first prize at the bike show, but he had just blown five of it, in five days, half of that, was what he knew he spent, but the other half, was what the woman had left with, except for a lonely, hundred dollar bill that was lying on the table with a quick note saying that breakfast, lunch and dinner was on her.

She also said, that she had to get back to work, really missed her kids and was sending most of the money out to her old man, so that he could get his rig back on the road and then hopefully meet-up with him in L.A.

She thanked him for it all of course, and then as a post script, she said that she'd pay him back some day, but he definitely wasn't holding his breath over that one, and he certainly didn't remember giving her any of the money to begin with.

Never mind, it was a done deal now anyway, and it was time for him to scoot on down the road, so he put some music on his pocket radio and cranked up the throttle to both, the radio and his bike. It was going to be a good day and that was for sure.

****

Now one of the problems about being a biker is that you always have to travel in the weather. If it's raining, then you're bound to get wet. If the sun shines, you'll definitely feel it, and sometimes, it'll even burn you and if the wind's up, that affects the way you ride, and it often blows you off course, time after time. If you run into a storm, then you have to look for the nearest overpass, underpass, tree, farmyard or barnyard door, that's been left open, just to wait it out in, but on a great day, when the weather is fine, you can reach right up and touch the sky, just like the song says, and that's when you feel like you're riding somewhere in-between heaven and hell and there's no doubt about it my friend, all in all, it ain't a bad way to travel, but then you can never count on the weather now, can you?

Take that morning for instance; he decided to give himself eighteen hours to get back to Tulsa, even though he knew that he could probably make it back there in twelve, especially if he pushed it.

It was about eight hundred miles and pushing it would mean cranking the throttle wide-open for most of the way. He didn't like riding that way anymore, which is why he rode a chopper to begin with, and not a crotch rocket, or a road racer, or whatever else you want to call those bloody death machines.

He'd seen too many riders go down on them, and usually for their own stupid mistakes, like going too damn fast to begin with, but don't get me wrong, he still liked to fly and he loves speed, but he aint going to do that for twelve hours straight anymore, those days are long gone and besides that, who can afford the extra gas you use, not to mention the wear and tear on the motor and the risk of losing your license.

He used to have about a dozen of those, at one point in time, almost one for every State he travelled through on a regular basis, Texas, Oklahoma, Arkansas and Mississippi, in one direction, and Colorado, Nevada, California, Oregon and Washington, in another, and there were the three Canadians and a Mexican license that he had as well.

It was just the thing to do back then and to be honest, it was a lot cheaper to buy a license than it was to pay for a speeding ticket, but that all changed with personal computers. Licenses became national, and then international, so it didn't matter anymore where you were, they could see what tickets you had from any State or Province and they could also read up on your entire life story and access the other details as well, like how many times you've been arrested, for whatever reasons and when or where that was.

Yeah, times had changed that's for sure, but that was then and this was now, so he just figured that it was such a nice day, with blue skies and high temps, he could easily cruise for hours and that the sun would be with him most of the way back, but little did he know, although there was that ominous sort of feeling again, somewhere deep-down inside of him.

****

First of all there was an accident on the freeway just up ahead. It involved three cars and a jack-knifed rig that had no business being out there in the first place.

Now, I know what you're thinking, and no, it wasn't her. He wouldn't wish that on anyone, not even another thief just like her, but it had certainly killed a few people and then it mangled up a few more, just for good measure, you might say.

Apparently, the driver had been drinking and popping those Mexican Christmas trees, like they were going out of style. He also had some pink ladies, purple hearts and a large bottle of black beauties on him as well, which was more than enough speed, to keep him awake for at least a month at a time, if he hadn't mixed it with that bottle of Johnny Walker that is, which they found at the scene.

Who really knows how long he had actually been up, or even how long it took him to cross the border in the first place?

They said he was headed to New York City, which was a solid four or five day drive for a big rig like that, if not longer, so it was bound to happen, sooner or later and maybe this was better than what could've, would've, should've been. You just never know?

Anyway, they closed up the highway in all directions because of that and even though Billy was on a bike, he couldn't get passed the cops that had it all blocked off. So for the next two hours he sat there in traffic, patiently waiting it out, with the sun shining high above him once again, which eventually crept right up over his head. Oh well, at least it was moving this time, he thought.

Then, when the way was finally cleared, those bloody cops decided to hold him back for a little while longer, just long enough to run a make on his bike they said, and to do a safety check on it as well. Of course they also decided to run his name through their computers while they were at it, for good measure of course. So, it was another hour and half wasted after all that.

He should've turned back around right then and there. He should've gone back to that hotel room and found another woman to spend some time with, or at least hit a few bars and a good restaurant, but he had already decided that he had to go on regardless, he had people to see, places to go and things to do, you know how it is.

So, there he was finally, cruising at about seventy five miles an hour or more, when he saw this ominous dark cloud up over the horizon. Yeah, that's right, he was heading straight into a thunderstorm and it was looking pretty damn grim, but then, as his luck would have it, all of a sudden, it just got worse.

A long tail in the cloud started developing and he could see that it would probably drop, right down on top of him, if he wasn't careful. He was heading north at the time and he knew that turning around was out of the question.

What he really needed, was to get passed it all somehow, or at least find himself somewhere safe to wait for awhile, until the worst of it was over, like an overpass or underpass, if possible.

Now, we're not talking about a little Texas twister here, no, this was a full blown, category three or four tornado and it was coming right at him.

A little rain and some bad weather won't usually hurt anyone too much, but this thing could get deadly for hundreds of people, if it came down the right way, or even the wrong way, it doesn't really matter and believe you me, when I say that it looked as if, it was about to come down right on top of him.

He was back in the desert by then, with nowhere to run and nowhere to hide. He didn't have any choice really, it was find another direction to go, like turning east or west, or simply ride on through it. Unfortunately, there wasn't any other road to take and out running it, wasn't going to be an option, because it never is. These things can travel up to three hundred miles an hour at times and they can lay a path of destruction for mile after mile depending on how long they touch down.

Some people say that they'll tear up fifty miles or more around them. But he sure as hell wasn't waiting to find out. So, he cranked up his throttle from seventy five to eighty, eighty to ninety, and then ninety to one twenty. Was he crazy or what?

He was riding like a bat out hell, heading straight for it and sure enough he was right on the money. The damn thing was touching down in front of him, ripping the bushes apart along the side of the road and throwing up dirt and debris all over the place, including him, but he wasn't stopping for no-one, he was going to ride right on through it; at least that's what he thought he'd do.

Now, it was pretty hard for him to know exactly what happened next, because it all became surreal; and to be honest, he just doesn't know what really happened. Did he crash, or did he pull over to wait it out? He honestly doesn't remember, but what he does remember, is that everything seemed to be slowing down at the time, and then somehow, it all just stopped, as if he'd been trapped in a time warp, or something else that was just as strange and as twisted as you could ever imagine.

The worst thing about it, was the fear that he had lost his hearing through it all, because one minute, the sound was louder than a freight train smashing into the side of a mountain and the next minute, it was completely silent, as if someone had simply reached up and pulled out both of his eardrums at the same time.

He was still on his bike though, at least that's what he thought, but the road wasn't there anymore. In fact, nothing was there anymore; it was simply another world, as if he had been beamed up by some freaky alien in a spaceship, like the ones you see in a bad Star Trek movie.

He finally realized, that his bike wasn't running at the time, and that he wasn't moving at all. Not up, down or sideways, not straight ahead or even backwards, in fact nothing was moving, there wasn't anything there left to move.

He didn't know what to do, so he just got off the bike and found out that he was standing on thin air, only he couldn't see it and his bike was standing there, all by itself as well, without the aid of its kick stand.

He decided that he must have died, and that all of this was some sort of limbo, like purgatory, or nirvana, and that's when he heard that old familiar voice, calling out to him again, somewhere in the darkness, and not too far off, in the distance.

"Hello Billy" the voice said, but he couldn't see a damn thing standing there, so eventually he just yelled out,

"Here I am old man, what do you want with me this time and where in the hell are you?" Of course, he immediately knew, that it was that crazy old man again, after all, who else would it have been? You know the one I'm talking about, the one that he had met in the desert just a few days before. He was probably the devil in all reality, he had to be, but he looked just like any other old man, to Billy anyway.

"Well here you are again, the old man said; fancy meeting up here like this? You've gone and done it good and proper this time, haven't you? You should have turned off when you had the chance, instead of heading straight for me."

"I guess so, old man; he said, rather quick and impatiently, so what now? Where do we go from here?"

"That depends on you my boy, the old man said, where do you want to go?"

"Well, I was heading to Tulsa and that's where I really want to go, but surely you already know that?"

"Oh yeah, he said, I actually do know that, and to Tulsa you shall go, eventually, but first I want you to do something for me?"

"Why me, he said again, what could I possibly do for you old man?"

"Oh, you'll see soon enough my boy; the old man said, laughing with that stupid eerie laugh that he's always had. You see, now you're one of my "Angels" and I have a need for all of my Angels at this very moment in time. There's a war going on, and I need all the help that I can get."

"Wait a minute Billy said, you know that I've already done my time fighting for the cause, I don't need any more of that bullshit and besides, I'm too old for that now, so why don't you go and get yourself a younger man, you know the type, one with no brains, no worries, and no doubts, and maybe a ton of muscle, if you're lucky. I'm sure that you could find a few of those out here, easy enough."

"Ha, ha, the old man said, and here I thought you were the hero type. Don't worry about it Billy, just do it. I'll be here to hold your hand if necessary, he said, still laughing."

"Don't get me wrong here old man, I don't need any ones hand to hold thank you very much, but I sure as hell don't appreciate being shanghaied either. So let's just get on with this business, so that I can get back to my life and away from you for good. This sort of inconvenience just pisses me off and I'm about fed up with being pissed off right now, if you know what I mean, particularly by you."

"That's the spirit my boy, the old man said, I knew that you wouldn't let me down, especially after I saved your life, only a few days ago."

"Oh yeah, go ahead and take the credit for that will you, I said, after all it was you that put me in the middle of that mess in the first place. I spent a lot of money on that bike, just to have you screw it up, like you did."

"Yeah well, I gave it all back to you and then some if you remember right, so don't come complaining to me about it Billy boy and by the way, how was that sweet looking truck-driver anyway, she certainly was a pretty little thang

~ 211 ~

wasn't she?" he said, smiling even bigger than what he normally did.

"Speaking of money, Billy said, quickly, changing the subject, what's a gig like this going to be worth to me then? I figure that it has to be worth quite a lot, especially, if I have to kill all the bad guys and save the frigging world etc."

"Here we go again, the old man said, always looking for that almighty dollar. It's not as if I couldn't do this without you now is it? You would think that you'd just want to do it for the shear hell of it, if you get the pun, after all, it's not every day that you get to go to where we're going and then come back from it all, now is it?"

"So I have to agree to all of this then, right, he quickly said, otherwise you really can't force me to do anything, can you?"

"Well, I could just keep you where you're at right now, with no problems, the old man said, and you never would get back to Tulsa or anywhere else for that matter, life could suddenly become pretty boring, hanging around here all by yourself."

"Ok, ok, I get the picture, but I still want the money, it's not like it's off your back or something, all you have to do is conger it up like you did before and then all I have to do is spend it," he said, with a really big smile, on his own face.

"Hahaha, the old man said, that's not a problem Billy boy, when it's all finished you'll be a rich man for a little while, and you have my word on that."

Then, they went through the motions of shaking hands again, only this time it was all too real. He could actually feel the old man's hand this time, and it didn't feel so good to him. It was kind of cold and clammy, almost like shaking hands with a corpse. It sent a shiver down his spine and he immediately wiped his hand on his jeans afterwards. He also realised that he should have stated just how much money was involved to begin with, but he didn't. Oh well, it was done deal by then, he figured.

The next thing that he knew, he was being sucked into the very depths of the earth itself, somewhere into a deep, dark pit, like place, filled with absolutely nothing and there he was all of a sudden, sweating his nuts off again, trying to make sense of it all and also trying to plug my ears from the God awful sounds that he was hearing which were agonizing screams of complete and utter misery that simply surrounded us, no matter which way we turned.

The place was more than you could imagine, let alone hope to write about. It was truly horrible, to say the least, indescribably horrible in-fact. The only thing that lit it up, were the fires that seemed to be burning everywhere, especially the ones that were burning everyone in and around them.

Some of them, were up in the air, suspended on their own somehow, floating around, while on fire, at the same time, it was kind of like staring at stars, only not as good. The closest that you could come to a complete description of it all, would be one gigantic cave, buried deep, somewhere in the centre of the earth maybe, or perhaps a different dimension altogether?

You could see for miles, in every direction though, and mile after mile, there were fires, along with indescribable beings, living or half living, or completely dead, he didn't know which, but all of them were being tossed and turned every which way he looked, in what seemed to be pure agony, in one way, shape or another. And then there was the smell of it all, an overwhelming putrid stench, the smell of certain death that filled his nostrils and lungs to the point of suffocation. It was definitely not the place that you would want to book a family holiday to, that's for sure, and he wanted to leave as soon as he got there, but naturally he knew, that it wouldn't be an option for him. He had to ride it out, no matter what it took.

"So, he finally said, as they walked along, what is it that I'm supposed to do down here old man? What is it that you really want from me?"

"Well, the old man said, now that you're here; let me tell you what you'll really need to know. So listen up now, because I don't want to have to repeat myself. You see, today, you are the chosen one, thanks to yours truly that is. Every power that you'll ever need is at your finger tips. Infact, all of the powers of the universe are deep down inside of you right now at this very moment in time, as we speak.

You are everything that I am, perhaps even more and before you, out there in the emptiness, lie's the battle ground, along with an army of such immensity, intensity and mass, that no-one has ever seen the likes of it before, no-one, you can take my word for that, and it all waits there for you and you alone. It's the perfect killing machine, of all ages, with warriors that will never die, no matter how many times they get shot, stabbed or blown into little bits and pieces.

After all, you can't kill something that's already dead and believe me when I say that they are all dead, they're beyond dead, they're as dead as dead can get and all you have to do is take control of it, take control of them and then make it all work for you, make it do your bidding, as you desire." And then the old man said, "The object of it all is to win the war of course, the war that will be waged here in no time at all."

"So, who are we fighting?" Billy said, as if he didn't already know the answer.

"What you and your kind have always referred to as God of course, the old man said, as he laughed out loud again, it's always God and it always has been."

"Well isn't that a little strange, Billy said again, because if you're always fighting God and he's the one that made you to begin with, along with everything else that there ever was, then how in the world could you ever expect to win a war against him?"

"I don't expect to win Billy, I expect you to win, the old man said, still laughing, it's all down to you now; you're the man for the job, trust me, I'm never wrong."

"I still don't get it, he said, how could I ever expect to beat God? From what I understand, he's the beginning of everything I know, and the end of everything else, and there's nothing that anyone could ever do to change that, because if they did, it would simply put an end to all that there is, and we wouldn't have anything to fight about anyway, because we wouldn't exist.

We would be nothing, nothing at all without God; it's as simple as that. You should know this old man, what's the matter with you? Where's your head at?"

"You mean to tell me, that a bad assed biker like yourself actually believes in all that bullshit then? You mean to say that you're really afraid of God?" the old man said, pointing his finger at him and shaking it.

"No old man, I'm not saying that at all. I'm not afraid of God; I'm not afraid of dying either and I'm certainly not afraid of you. It's just that I have respect for God and for what he is, just as I have respect for you and for what you are, along with everything else, for what it is as well. To me, there's simply no point in going to war against the one that created "War" to begin with, the one that created everything that there ever was, and everything that there ever will be and in-fact, the only being that truly exists. To me, a war with God, is actually a war against myself, because without God, there wouldn't be any me to begin with, now would there?"

The old man started laughing again, only this time it wasn't his usual laugh, this time it was a whole lot softer and slightly sweeter than it usually was

Then he started fading from Billy's sight, disappearing slowly, right in front of his eyes, while the fires of hell, that were burning all around them to begin with, suddenly started going out one by one, and the cave that they were in, simply opened up to the heavens above and a great star, brighter than any that he had ever seen before, sat there high above it all.

He turned to the old man again and saw how he had changed his appearance. He was younger now more agile, taller and much thinner. He also had long flowing white hair, a clear complexion and no scars on his face anymore.

It was almost like looking into a mirror for Billy, with a reflection of his father, or something, if that makes any sense, looking right back at him, except for the fact, that he was all dressed up in white and had something around him that glowed, shining like the stars above.

"You seem to have become pretty wise in your years, Billy, the man standing next to him said, and it seems that you may have finally seen the truth of things, and all I can do, is expect you to go back into the world and tell that truth, to whomever may listen. When you've finished telling all that you can tell, then we'll meet again and you'll become part of me again, as you truly are now, for I am you and you are me and we are all that there ever was, and all that there will ever be. Because without you there is no me and without me, there is no you.

So, go my son and rest assured that your troubles are over for awhile. Find your peace in the world of the living and try to live a good life; try to keep up with good will towards all of mankind, for they are within you as well, as they are within me. We are all one with everything, as everything is always one with us."

It was a pretty profound moment to say the least, as he stood there realizing the meaning behind it all, finding himself in awe by this supernatural beings presence, along with his mannerisms and his mild tone of voice. He also realized at that moment in time that he was completely and utterly at peace with himself, in such a way, that he had never experienced before. He knew right then and there, that what the old man was saying, was probably one of the greatest truths that he had ever heard, and he also knew, that he had finally come home, and that he never wanted to leave home again, but then, he didn't have a choice in the matter, just like any other time and he knows that he still doesn't.

Suddenly, he was sitting on his bike again, along the side of the highway that he was travelling down earlier, before the tornado hit him. The younger old man was standing there with him.

"Close your eyes Billy, the old man said; imagine yourself floating backwards through space and time which really doesn't exist. All of your yesterdays are gone; all of your teenage years, your childhood years and even your infancy.

Close your eyes and see yourself, before you were even born to this life. Before you were in your mother's womb, before you were a twinkle in your father's eye.

Then see yourself, a hundred years before that, as another person that once walked this earth as you do today.

Then quickly go backwards to a thousand years ago and then go back to a million until finally, you'll see yourself as part of the great abyss that has always been there and will always be there.

Relax now and take all of it in, because this is where we all started. This is where we come from. This is the beginning of all there ever was and at the same time, it is also the end.

In the beginning there was the word and the word was God. Now, this isn't about Christianity Billy, but Christ himself found out these same answers long before they nailed him to the cross. And since that time, billions of people on this planet have read it or they have been told about it, for thousands of years or more and still, they don't have a single clue, as to its true meaning."

Nevertheless we all have our beginnings and it is to that beginning that I shall go to next. Relax and come with me, it won't take us long."

Billy just sat there on his bike listening intently to what the old man was saying. He'd never been religious before and he certainly wasn't going to change his ways now, but what this old man was saying, made perfect sense to him and besides that, it wasn't about religion in any way, shape or form, it was about something that was far beyond all of that. It was the secret to life itself.

He could only hope that he was making sense of it all, but perhaps it was far beyond his limited comprehension, so he could only write what he remembered; and pray that he got it right?

****

"***In the beginning there was Emptiness, the old man said,*** a cold, distant, dark and lonely place, completely void of any light, sound, sense, or reason. No shape, no substance, nothing but a big black hole, caught up in the deep, dark recesses of a non-existence. Then for whatever reasons out of the emptiness, there came a single thought." "I am"

Once that happened, I am, started thinking other thoughts, which quite miraculously, just seemed to flow out of "I am" at that single moment in time.

Some would say that it was a sudden sense of awareness, but that's all debatable, anyway, "I am" realized that he/she/it was, and it was as simple as that; therefore "I am" said to itself, I am and I shall always be, everything that I am.

Eventually and always thinking, I am realized that there was more to think about and so much more to do than "I am" could ever do alone, and soon "I am" decided not to be alone, ever again." So "I am" split it-self into two parts and these two parts became "We." We are, therefore we shall always be all that we can be, because we are.

For awhile, perhaps millions or billions of years, or perhaps, it was only a few seconds, in the grand scheme of things, this was the way things were. We are, therefore we will be, but we are, also realized that there was more to be achieved, so much more to be done as well, so the second part of "I am" split itself again and the three parts became known as "they."

The two had become three. They are and therefore, they shall always be, we are and so we shall always be, I am and I will always be. Not long after that, the two parts that split again and they became them."

"I am" we are, they are, them and then it was you. You, them, they, we, "I am"

All that ever was, is and will always be, multiples of "I am." It's as simple as that my boy and I do hope that you're following all of this because there's a lot more to it than that.

Long before life came to this planet; there was already life in the outer regions of what we now call space and time.

The heavens were full of life, but it wasn't quite like the life that we know now, and obviously, it wasn't anything like it at all. A true description of what that life was at that particular moment in time would be impossible to put into words, but I believe that the time has come for you to try and understand it.

The thought was pure and simple. "I am," it was neither a question nor an answer, but simply a statement.

"I am" became "We are", multiples of itself, by splitting itself into two. This in turn was multiplied again, and it became they are, over and over and over again.

There really isn't any, "they" or "we", for truly all there is, is "I am." You are I am. They are I am. We are I am. I am I am. Everything that ever was, has always been and will always be, "I am."

Now let me tell you what you already know, Billy, because you've forgotten all about it through the years and the many lives that you've lived before. I am the father, the grand-father and the great-grandfather of Quicksilver, whose multiple legions were of the planet Mars. I have lived a thousand lifetimes and many more, and I will continue to live until the end of all that there ever was.

I have taken many shapes and many forms over the centuries, and I have been known by many different names. I am on this earth, as I have been for thousands of years, waiting for the time that has finally come.

Hear me speak and mark my words, because the world that you know is finally changing and what it is today will soon be no longer. And what it was before will ultimately be again.

I am a being of light; I am the first and the last of the multiples of my kind. "I am" "We are" "They are" etc.

My kind rules the heavens and the earth, the planets and the stars and everything that truly lies in-between. They brought everything into existence. We brought everything into existence. I brought everything, into existence.

Now hear these words, my son and hear them well.

When this earth was formed long ago, a great canopy was placed around it. We called that canopy the misty ring and it surrounded the earth, much as the Ozone layers do today. However, the misty ring was miles thick and yet, it was still quite transparent and it gave all below it, complete protection, from all of everything that was above it. Not much different to a mother's womb, it nurtured everything within it.

Plants grew in great abundance and everything flourished. Animals fed extremely well, which in turn, allowed them to grow into incredible sizes, and every man, woman, and child, that walked this earth, started out living, just as long as they wanted to, or wished for.

There was no death, no sickness, no such thing as disease and no need for war, and there was never any famine.

There wasn't an ageing population either, people grew-up, but they never grew old. A thousand years was simply like twenty or thirty years today, as far as body growth goes.

Everyone was fit and healthy and all was good here, infact, all was very well in the gardens of "Pangaea" or this Earth, as it's known today.

The legions of light, (multiples of "I am") had split the darkness in the heavens for all time, sitting Pangaea, along with eleven other planets, in the middle of a space that circled a great star that you earthlings now call the sun."

The sun gave up its light and reigned down its energy, to all of the planets and it was good for a very long time. Everything was, as it came to be, until finally, the thought wars in the heavens started.

That's when the legions of the sky had grown restless, through the millenniums of time. The thought was that it wasn't any good to exist anymore, without being able to actually feel that existence. The multiples had no feelings; they were simply beings of light, made from pure energy, with no earthly form, or any real shape.

They had no bodies, no solid mind to speak of and no kind of soul to nurture; they were just pure light, pure energy and pure thought."

So it came to pass, that some of them, had seen humankind develop on Pangaea, and had decided that it would be good to live like man and to take on man's daughters for wives of their own, and to create their own offspring. But in order to do this, they would have to become the same as man, simply because, a being of

Pangaea, could never become a being of the sky, nor of the heavens.

The two were simply and completely, incompatible with each other, as they have always been and of course, they will always be. Mankind has been made of the earth and of the earth, is where they will always remain.

All the beings of light, who chose to ground, would have to sacrifice everything that they were in the heavens, for who, or what it was, that they wanted to be, here on earth. It was known as the great sacrifice, but in the long run, it was also a very foolish one. Eventually the thought, was erased from the minds of those that chose to ground. Causing them to forget where it was, that they actually came from to begin with.

Most of them were happy enough to do so anyway, except that it was no longer meant for them to live forever in one simple existence, now they had to exist time after time. In doing this, we changed the course of humankind as well, because now, man could no longer exist forever neither, they had to die, in order for us to die.

At first that life span was over a thousand years. A thousand years was plenty enough time for all of us to experience all that we wanted or needed to experience, during that lifetime, but soon that just became old hat and new experiences were needed. More and more of the multiples wanted to experience this existence as well, until all of humankind, was basically possessed, by all of the multiples in the heavens.

Now, I'll tell you a little secret Billy, before I leave you once again, the old man said, You won't remember the rest of what I said anyway, because it's locked up so deep, inside of your subconscious mind, that it simply won't ever come out, and in the long run, it doesn't really matter anyway, because you are, who you are and you will do what you do, regardless.

I hope you remember this, because it's the most important thing to remember in this life and probably the most important thing that I could ever tell you.

Everything that we go through in life, affects us. Everyone we meet, everyone we even think about, wish for, and desire, has an effect on us from birth, right up until death, and all of the time in-between."

Grandparents, parents, uncles and aunts, friends, relatives, strangers, siblings and grandchildren, are all continuations of the life that we live, as we are, in the lives that they live as well. Whether we know those people or not, whether they are even real or not, they are still a part of us. What we are to them and what they are to us is what truly what makes us who we are, and there's more.

Water, earth, wind, fire, the sky, the Sun and the Moon, plants, animals, insects, the stars and the planets themselves, all affect us in one way or another, whether we can see that or even feel it, doesn't matter, it's always been that way, right from the beginning of time."

However, what makes us individual, set apart from everyone and everything else that there is in this world, is our ability to reason, pro-create and perceive, the absolute truth behind all of that thought. Perception is everything, alongside, our own emotions. Love, hate, envy, happiness, despair, sadness, loneliness etc, these are the things that also make us truly unique, because no-one has our specific thought patterns and feelings, although some people may share those thoughts and feelings with us from time to time, but in reality, they are yours and theirs alone.

What you like or dislike, what you find funny or sad, can be found in others, don't get me wrong, it's just that how funny, is funny to you? And how sad, is sad to them? Or vice versa, and it gets better than this.

When it all gets down to it, in the end, it is really plain and simple Perception.

What we perceive, is what we think reality, really is and the truth of that matter is, that we all have separate reality's, every single one of us, from the beginning of our lives, up until the end of it and of course, every second of that life in-between."

How is it all possible, that's really quite simple as well? There is no such thing as life for a being of light. We exist; have always existed but only live when we take on earthly forms. However, life is only a thought and the perception of that thought made by us to explain something that has yet to be explained.

Now, you're probably lost to what it was that I've just said, after all, how could that be, when we are all living, breathing creatures, you might just ask?"

So, let me explain it to you as simply as I can. We exist as we always have, from the beginning to the end, but the perception of that existence, changes, as we allow it to and others have the will to change it as well.

What we're going through is a continuation of our own existence. A perception that we've created, that allows us to feel our own emotions, which in truth, is necessary for the benefit of our existence.

We can always change our perception, as we so often do and we can allow others to change it for us, which is more often the case, but in order to change it completely, we have to go back to the very beginning, when that first perception, first came into our existence, in other words, when thought, first became thought.

That, my friend, is what is known as *Shamaiya.* (Our initial thought)

Knowing that we exist, what that existence is, and knowing how to change it all, at will. This then becomes Shamaiya as well (only it's the way that we exist.)

****

Shamaiya is our existence, our way of life and when you finally arrive at or into the final stages of *Shamaiya,* (which is Death, for want of a better word) then all the answers, to all of the questions, that have ever been asked, will be yours to do as you wish."

That is known, as the *Ultimate Shamaiyan experience*, a complete awareness of the beginning and the end, of all that there ever was, all that was ever perceived and all that there has ever been.

You are Shamaiyan Billy, from the beginning of it all up until the end of it all.

Shamaiyans are true multiples of "I am" Shamaiya, is simply the beginning and the end of that absolute truth.

The old man cackled again, just as he had so many times before. His appearance was back to his older self, the one that Billy had met in the desert to begin with.

It's time that I got back, my boy, you won't remember half of what I told you anyway, and time is waiting for no one.

You've got all you need for awhile and we will eventually meet up again, there's no doubt about that. You have yourself a great trip back to Tulsa; I really don't think that there will be too many problems ahead of you for awhile, but do keep it upright and in-between the lines this time, because you never know what's around the corner." and with that, the old man was gone.

****

The sun was shining, the grass was green, and the skies were crystal blue and clear. Billy looked down at his saddle bags again and saw that they were stuffed full of cash, one hundred dollar bills, just like before.

What a great day, he thought, as he started up his motorcycle. Then he sniffed the air, took a good look around, liked what he saw and with that, he scooted off, like a man on a mission, one more time.

****

Post script

Now I don't want people to think that I'm trying to convert them into some kind of religion here or trying to install a thought process that they really have no idea about and could care less about anyway. Because I'm definitely not, you can trust me on that. After all, I'm just a writer and I don't do religion, as I've said before.

So what I've written in the last two stories, are only words and that's what they should be regarded as. What you believe and what I believe will always be two different things, no matter what, and there's nothing wrong with that, everyone should have their own opinions, their own mind, their own thought processes etc.

So yeah, Billy was out there in the Texas desert, and yeah, he got himself bitten by some fire ants, and yeah, he was picked up by a woman truck driver and spent a week with her in a hotel room, and most of all, he had some strange experiences, that he couldn't explain, but you believe what you want to believe, after all, I'm only writing a story here.

There'll be more about Billy Lee Brixton as this story unfolds, but right now I'm going to get more personal again and give you another glimpse of the life I've lived, so enjoy.

****

16
The Hotel

I was barely nineteen at the time, going on fifty, and feeling every bit of it, when I stepped down from the dark-side of a murky-grey, un-marked military jet, late in the summer of the early Seventies, feeling ratted, tattered, frazzled and fried. Psychologically damaged maybe, but temporarily repreived, from fighting in a war that was nobody's business in the first place, let alone mine.

Laos, Cambodia, and Viet-Nam, were thousands of miles away from where I grew-up and about a million miles away from where I really wanted to be, but it was their time to shine in the spotlight of the Worlds Stage, and I was just another actor, that had been sucked into playing his part in that particular movie. I just didn't realize it would turn out to be such a bloody horror story.

Now don't get me wrong here, I wasn't complaining about any of it. I know that we do whatever we have to do in this life, and I was pretty damn good at doing what I did. In-fact, I figured that I was one of the best of the best, and if the truth were ever known, I loved every minute of it anyway and I definitely wouldn't have traded it for the world.

There's something about a war that brakes you as you once were, and then it makes you as you need to be, and there's no in-between any of that, no going back neither. Because when it's done, it's definitely done and dusted.

Hell, I had even signed up for it all to begin with, grabbing the bull by the horns so to speak, riding high upon its crooked back, instead of being stomped into the ground by one of its heavy, cloven-hooves, or maybe pinned to the wall by one of its horns? And let's face it; I trained long and hard for that fucking privilege and for every mission that I was ever on, making sure that I got the highest marks available, out every bit of Intel, testing, training and prep, that they could throw at me in the first place, while at the same time, I always tried to keep myself at a distance, slightly above and a little beyond, the rest of the rank and file, doing whatever it took, to get to wherever it was that I needed to get to, just as quickly as I could, and very few of them knew, that I was as young as I was at the time, in-fact the truth is, most of them didn't know that at all.

It certainly wasn't easy though, in-fact it was just the opposite most of the time, but I thought I was out to change the world back then and I was giving it my best shot.

I had lied about my age to begin with, so that I could get involved earlier on, changing a six into a four on a piece of paper, which allowed me to join the army at the age of fifteen, instead of seventeen, and I'm pretty sure that I wasn't the only one who did that and besides, I had lied about my age for most of my life anyway, always telling people that I was a couple of years older than what I really was, especially when it came to the fairer sex. Older women, you've got to love em.

Some say I was a natural, young, fit, healthy and tough, with a strong will and an ambitious mind that was usually smart as a whip and often just as quick. But there were others that said, that I was dangerous, quick-tempered, unprepared, gun-ho, often obtuse, and I guess that somehow, all of that added up the fact that I was heading towards an early demise, according to them anyway.

I'd like to think that I was more compassionate than what most people gave me credit for, especially for the work that I did and some of the things that I had to go through back then, always hoping that someday, I'd actually make a difference to this world, in the long run that is. But I was too immature for all of that, and pretty damn naïve with it as well, never quite realizing that the long run, would actually be the rest of my life, and that making any kind of difference to this world or any other world for that matter, would never mean the same thing to anyone else, especially to my older self, whenever I got to it, if I ever got to it that is? Never mind, that's just the way life had been for me, and it don't matter anyway. It never has and it never would.

****

Once I stepped onto the tarmac, I was immediately confronted by a group of extraordinarily overbearing people that came at me from out of nowhere?

You know the kind that I'm talking about, left-wing, liberal, pacifists/tree-hugger types, shouting obscenities from the top of their lungs, on the sidelines of course, like baby-killer, child-rapist, drug-dealer, war–monger, fascist and cold-blooded murderer, amongst other niceties that they were coming out with.

Ignorant little pricks, full of self-importance, self-entitlement and self-worth, that didn't know their ass from a hole in the ground, and they certainly didn't have the brainpower between them to figure it out.

They were the cancel society of the day, which are no different to those around now, over-educated, over-fed, over-pampered and over-paid, if any of them have actually held a job at all, and yet, not a single ounce of decency or common sense between the lot of them.

They threw things at me, while they were stomping on flags, burning them or simply tearing them apart and spitting into the air, trying really hard to hit me with it, and I swear that if I was armed at the time, I would have just shot the lot of them, right there on the spot, for being the pathetic little turncoat traitors, that they appeared to be. I didn't suffer fools gladly, that's for sure, especially that kind of fool.

I suppose I'm over that now, after all, it was over fifty years ago, and I've been through a lot of life since then, but there are those that I've known, that never did get over it, and there were too many more, that didn't actually survive it all to begin with.

I still feel for them, I hold em in my memories, I see them in my dreams at times, but that's what a bullshit fucking war does to people. Who would've thought? In-fact, every war that was ever fought, has turned out to be just as bad. It splits the country down the middle, dividing the North from the south and the east from the west.

Pitting brother against brother and father against son, and it's never the same afterwards, no matter who you are, no matter where it happens in the first place?

I guess that some people might just call that progress, but I tend to think, it's a step backwards in time. To too many darker days and forgotten periods in our history, where the rich and greedy, take everything from the poor and the needy, then, simply kill the ones that weren't strong enough to object, or survive it all in the first place.

It happens all the time and it's still happening today. Infact it's been going on that way for thousands of years, and no-one seems to be able to stop it. But worse than that, is the fact that no-one really cares about it anyway.

It's just the nature of the beast or the devil down inside, or the plain and simple fact, that we as human beings, have that killer instinct, buried deep down inside our own psyche's, waiting to let it loose at the drop of a hat, and it really makes me wonder how in the world, that we as a people, a race, or even a species, have ever survived this long in the first place?

Those so-called citizens; didn't know me from Adam of course. They didn't know who I was, where I'd been or what I was about at all. Hell, they didn't even know, if I had served in the same war that they were protesting against, but I was wearing a uniform at the time, and that was all it took to set em off, regardless of what had really happened, way back when and to whom? But the worst part about it was the fact that they didn't give a shit about any of it, anyway.

They had their own agendas going on, regardless of what that actually was, or what they thought it was to begin with, and all I was, was just another dumb, semi-useless, farm animal, that somehow, managed to escape from the slaughter house that people like them, and their self-righteous kind, had actually created in the first place. What a fucking joke?

So there I was, completely worn-out, torn-up and broken down from the life that I'd been living, up to that point in time anyway. In-fact, it had been pretty well, full on, for too long really, but I was undeniably grateful that I was still alive, even though it seemed like I was only hanging on by a thread.

I immediately thought about a place to go for awhile, like a motel or a hotel, because where I had been and what I'd gone through during the past couple of years, was what most people's idea of what "Hell on earth", would look like, and what I needed now, more than anything else, was to try and forget everything that I could, about any of it.

I still belonged to the military of course, but I was also a biker with ties, and I planned to reconnect with some of them, just as soon as I could, before my next posting got in the way of that, and to keep things sweet with the club, if nothing else.

I also wanted to scoot, get laid and of course, catch up on all the news that I had missed out on, but most of all, I just wanted out of that damned uniform for awhile, have a nice taste of civy-street and mingle with some of the local yokels, especially the ones of the fairer sex.

I was flown into and processed out of McCord Air Force Base, with a little more time spent at Ft. Lewis, which is just up the road from McCord, but they sent me down to Elliot AFB afterwards and then eventually they shipped me up to Cheyenne Mountain, for a three day debriefing, that was like an inquisition instead of a fact-ending mission, and all of that was before I actually received my official furlough, so getting out of that uniform, had to wait.

Military clearance is a bitch at the best of times, especially if you've ever held any kind of high classification. I was basically on loan to the US for the duration of my contract, which wasn't up for a couple of more years, but still, it had to be done, and that was about all there was to that.

The closest club from there was up the road in Colorado Springs, which is neatly nestled high-up in the mountains, at somewhere just over four-thousand feet or so.

It's a little south of Denver and just off to the east of Interstate twenty-five, roughly midway through the State. It's basically a religious community, that was started-up during the gold rush days of the eighteen hundreds, filled with Protestants, Mormons, Jo-ho's and Catholics, all battling it out over whose word of God is the real one.

You know the story; it's just another bloody war that's been going on for a couple of thousand years. You'd think that most intelligent people would know better by now. I mean really, if God were to have any kind of religion, it sure as hell wouldn't be mans religion now, would it? And besides that, how many variations do you actually need on ten bloody rules, in the first place?

Of course I'd been there before, several times in-fact; I had stayed in Denver, before I went into the army, and Colorado Springs had always a pit stop along the way, so it was a local club for me, along with the fact that they had only been patched over a year or two before I went in the army, which still made them prospects and probates in my eyes. But before all of that, they were simply known as the Prophets, who would've thought?

Anyway, after a quick call, a few verbal ribs, along with some of laughs and a glad you made it back in one piece my friend, sort of thing, a few of the original Prophets, guys that I knew fairly well, including the "Dude" who ran them all, finally came and picked me up just outside the gates.

It was a warm summers evening, with a mild south western wind blowing-up a light breeze, in and around the area at the time, but to me, it was just what the Doctor ordered, and I was itching to scoot on out of there anyway, no matter what?

Eventually, I spent the night in Colorado Springs, camped out at the clubhouse, in the arms of a gorgeous, little hang-around that was also a full-on stripper at the local titty bar. She was a gift from the "Dude" who was the clubs president back then, and one of four, who had started up the original club in the first place.

I didn't mind at all, because the pair of us had hit it off together, pretty quick like. It was simply lust at first sight and all of that, you might just say. She was a looker though, that's for sure.

We had our fun drinking, laughing, kissing and smoking whatever was on the menu, and then we were simply screwing each other's brains out, in one of the back rooms, long before anyone else had even missed us. But I needed some hard, cold, down time, in order to be alone with my thoughts, my dreams and all of those bloody nightmares that I could never shake. So without too much persuasion, I borrowed a bike, and then I headed out of town alone, with my thoughts in tow, early the next morning.

A few short days at the most, is what I figured. I'd have to give the bike back by then anyway, simply because good ole Uncle Sam, and her Majesty's Military were still pulling my strings, and they simply wouldn't give me any more time off than that.

It was your typical bureaucratic bullshit really, no matter which way you looked at it, because I had at least a month's furlough coming to me by then, no matter what, but regardless of all of that, they would only dish it out in weekly increments, unless I went back to England of course, because of who I was or where I was, I suppose, no matter who I was with, or what I was actually doing at the time.

Now, don't get me wrong about this, because I had signed up for it all in the first place, but like I've said before, but I really didn't have a choice in the matter.

I'd gotten into all kinds of trouble in Germany a few years back when I was thirteen.

Lying about your age and trying to outsmart the system, doesn't ever do you any good and I ended up in a high security prison, right next door to a contract killer known as the "Dutchman" who had worked for some really powerful people back then.

In-fact, I was looking at spending quite a few years next to him in that prison at the time, until he decided to do me a huge favour, by making a few phone calls to one or more of his contacts about me, and my distinct abilities etc.

I guess he figured that he was never getting out of there, but there was still a chance that I could, with his help of course. He was certainly right about that, because they were there in no time at all really and I was freed from that life.

However, once that decision had been made, there was no turning back on it and it's not something that you can walk away from neither, those ties that bind, so to speak.

Now, one of the best things about being a biker, is that once you jump on that bike and scoot on down the road, you're back in your own little world again and there's no-one else there, unless you really want them to be that is.

You head out, to where ever you want, whenever you like, and there's no-one to tell you any different. No-one saying that you need to be here, there, or anywhere. No-one saying that you should be doing this or that, no-one at all.

Just you and that motor humming, as you're riding along with the wind, catching the sun, or simply flying down a road that you've never been on before, with the moon high-up above you as well at times.

It doesn't matter which one it is, it just feels like heaven either way, and that's about all there is to that.

A lot guys will simply go fishing, or maybe head down to their local pub every night, or even out to the nearest titty bar, or strip joint to relax and unwind, from whatever, whenever. They might even have a boy's night out once or twice a week, or perhaps a week-end hunting trip and camping, etc.

Some of them might even drop a bundle on a horse or two, or a dog race and then spend the next seventy-two hours complaining of their losses and wishing that they had bet on the other one instead. Some may even save up what few pennies they can earn and do several weeks away at a time, perhaps a few times a year even, but I was never into any of that. If I wasn't out riding, then all I needed was a roof over my head, with four cold walls and a semi-comfortable bed that I could crawl into at night, but of course, being overseas for as long as I had been, I hadn't had that kind of comfort or luxury, in a helluva long time.

I was anti-social, or anything of the sort; because I loved having company, especially with that stripper, who was a drop-dead gorgeous type of woman in every way, I might add, but it was always a case of time for me, because time itself, was my most valued commodity and I could never get enough of it, if you know what I mean?

Most of us don't, when it gets right down to it, but for me, it was pretty much an all consuming factor at that particular point in my life, because, I've always figured that I was living on borrowed time as it was.

There were just too many instances, that I had seen the end coming and yet I still kept on going, kind of like that bloody rabbit commercial on the TV and I guess that I was either too damn stupid or too damn stubborn, to actually lay down and die, but I also knew that one day I'd have to regardless, just not today. So, it was off to one of those motel/hotel rooms that I headed to next.

Why I left Colorado-Springs in the first place, along with that gorgeous stripper at the clubhouse, and then headed off into the city, like I did, well, I have no idea, apart from the ride itself of course, which, was the thing to do at that particular moment in time, I suppose? Never the less, there I was, pulling into the parking lot of an old, run down, motel/hotel, late in the afternoon.

It was a fairly tall building, somewhere near the city centre, with the hustle and bustle of a half a million people at the time, dashing around here, there, and everywhere, along with the constant traffic, that was also polluting up the very air that they all breathed, but I knew it would quieten down after hours and the smog would eventually lift or simply fade away.

That's when the skies would clear again, and for a few brief moments, it would seem like stepping back a hundred years or more, long before any of my troubles began.

Cities are like that, people live their lives out in the suburbs, and then commute to their twenty, forty or even sixty story office buildings, somewhere between the hours of nine to five, five days a week, sometimes six, which is something that I've never been interested in doing, but it is what most of the white collar types do these days.

You know the kind I'm talking about, ones with their five-thousand dollar, three-piece suits, two-thousand dollar shoes, three-hundred dollar shirts and hundred dollar neckties, along with their fancy gold watches, diamond wrist-chains and silver cigarette lighters, as well as their tricked out road cages, that usually cost more than half of their house to begin with.

Anyway, I checked in a little after four pm with no worries and no real problems, cash in hand, saddlebags for a suitcase and with my Desert Eagle strapped to my side. Army issued of course, after a medal and a promotion that I got, just before I came back stateside, and then I went up to my room, which was cosy enough, I suppose?

It had a bed, which was good, an old TV and a shower etc. along with windows that overlooked the parking lot where I could keep an eye out on my borrowed ride, from time to time. Not that I really needed to, after all it was a club bike and it was fully stamped, but still, you can't be too careful about these things. There's idiots everywhere, especially in the city.

Two or three nights of this I thought, and it should do just fine, although I had already paid for five nights in advance and in cash, like I said, which is the way I've always done things, after all, I really needed to relax and sleep, so that's what I did.

I woke up late in the evening after that, fairly hungry, still tired and very, very cold. The room itself was heated of course, but there was frost on the window, so I looked around for the thermostat and turned it up. It wasn't a new building at all, and it definitely wasn't insulated. None of them are, when you think about it, but what the hell I thought, this ain't winter yet, so the temperature will probably rise by ten am, regardless.

I certainly hoped so anyway; because I really didn't want to be riding through the snow on my short vacation, even if I was in the middle of the mile high city.

Now, it wasn't long before I made my way out to the streets that night, to check on the bike of course, and then to walk to the nearest restaurant, looking for that proverbial bite to eat.

Fortunately, I found an all-night diner within a few short blocks of the place that I was staying at, and it was one with hardly any other customers in it at that time, so the service was pretty quick and fairly efficient, although the food was a little less than desirable at best.

I was hungry though, so I just assumed that it was edible? I had a cup of coffee with an order of pancakes and a couple of sunny-side eggs, along with some rashers of bacon on the side. Not exactly an evening meal, but it would do for now, I thought.

I actually have simple tastes, when it comes to food these days. A few years of the army life, will usually do that to most people. Not because the C-rations were that bad, you understand, but when you run out of them, you have to make do with whatever you can get and you'd be surprised at what I'd been able to get in my life, both before and after my days with Uncle Sam and her majesty's service.

Anyway, I had just finished eating my meal, when I first noticed the kid. The girl was too young to be out at that hour of the night and not much to look at, although she was kind of pretty, in the strangest sort of way, but more of a scrawny little thing, that probably didn't weigh more than seventy pounds soaking wet, if that, and she definitely didn't know how to take care of herself yet.

Probably, not a day over twelve or thirteen, I figured, not really sure why I was bothered with it in the first place? And not quite five feet tall either. And the guy that she was sitting with, well, he definitely looked old enough to be her father, although he was a whole lot heavier and at least a foot and half taller than what she was, but fathers don't treat their daughters the way that he was treating her, no sir, they don't do that at all.

I sat there watching them both for awhile, as I drank my coffee; the man had started yelling at the girl to get back to work, saying that she had been taking too many breaks, and that she wasn't making him any money just sitting there on her fat little ass.

I could easily see where that led to pretty quick. This guy was just another low-life, scumbag, a gangster, wannabee pimp type, or what I had always known as a pedo-chicken-hawk, who was hanging onto his prey and this prey was obviously too young to know any better, in-fact, she was probably too damn young to know much about anything at all really.

Now I don't know how or why, but I do know that it's a shame when you realize just how many young women get themselves into that kind of trouble, long before they have a chance in life, but there you go, they do, and that's just about all there is to that. Half the time, I think that it must be that, me, me, me, type of scenario, where they think that world owes them something and that it simply revolves around them and nobody else. But the other half, well that can be just about as dark and dangerous, and as pure evil, as evil can get.

Those girls have no chance at all, because of scumbags just like this guy, that are sitting around every bloody corner, just waiting to catch them in the shadows, then casually, carefully, and usually fairly quickly lead them back their lairs. No different than a Spider to a Fly, or a Wolf to a baby Elk. But, it wasn't any of my business, so I just sat there for awhile, listening to this guy's bullshit, until the girl finally got herself up and left him sitting there, as she quickly stepped outside in the cool night air.

I got up a while later myself and headed towards the till, to pay my bill. The man just sat there, staring at me, as I went up to the counter and then he continued staring, when I walked out the door, giving me that cold, hard, say something if you dare asshole, kind of look, catching my eyes more than just once, brazenly staring right back at me, without even a twitch or a flinch. Which is not what the usual citizens of the world do in a situation like that, that's for sure.

I kept an eye on his movements, his breathing and even his heartbeat, with both eyes open behind my back, as I slowly passed him along the way. I didn't like this guy at all and I knew that he could feel that about me, because I have a habit of projecting my feelings outwards for some reason, and I've always known that almost anyone could feel that sensation in a matter of seconds, no matter how hard I'd try to conceal it. I also figured that this guy was nothing but trouble with a capitol T. from the day that he was born and there was very little doubt about that in my mind. After all, I'd seen trash, just like him throughout the years and I was bound to see a lot more eventually.

I suppose that its human nature as they say, but I really couldn't stand that part about people and I didn't see the point of even trying. Anyway, the guy just sat there, watching me, staring, as I slowly left the building, which was a good thing really, because I wasn't looking for any trouble at the time, I had had my share of that recently, which is another reason of why I checked into that hotel in the first place.

Things had been pretty hectic overseas, for quite awhile, as I've said before, and there were people that I knew, including a couple of my closest friends that had gotten killed along the way. I had come close myself, but I was used to it all by then, hell, I'd been at it for a few years, so I knew what to expect.

Besides that, it was time to rest up for awhile, and try to forget all about that shit, before I had to go back and do it all over again and I was looking forwards to that, resting up that is.

The girl was standing on the corner when I finally got to it, which was no surprise really, after all that's what her chicken-hawk pimp had told her to do, and that's when she asked me point blank, if I wanted a date.

I smiled at her, said "no thanks" rather quickly and then as a second thought or perhaps some simple curiosity, I asked her how old she was and of course, she told me that she was eighteen, which I already knew was a lie just by looking at her. "But, I could be any age you want, the girl said, I love make-believe, don't you? Do you like em younger or older than me?"

I quickly turned her down again by saying that I really wasn't interested, but the girl kept on, walking along with me, asking me a whole slew of questions, like where was I from? Where was I going? And what was I going to do, once I got there? She even asked me if I wanted to get high and then she asked me if I was gay, because I kept telling her no. I didn't lie to her, but I didn't want her company either, and no, I certainly wasn't gay.

Then she used that old plea-bargaining technique, you know the one, could you please help me out, because I need the money to pay some bills, or her man would start beating her up again.

I told her that the best thing for her was to get back home. Get away from there and that kind of life just as fast as her feet would carry her, but of course she said that she couldn't do that. Her man relied on her to make the money; they were in "Love" and they needed each other in this life, because they didn't have anyone else. Which of course, was just another bullshit lie as well?

That guy wasn't capable of loving anyone but himself, no matter who came along and besides that, he probably had a string of other girls out on every corner, working their little socks off, amongst other things, but maybe she really did love him, who knows? Love is blind, especially when you're too young to know what love really is.

I'd seen it all before, too many times in-fact. Hell, even some of the clubs that I had dealt with in the past, had done the same kind of things, which really disgusted me more than I ever said at the time.

Still, it was their business, not mine and if it ain't my business, then staying out of it, is usually the best way to go, unless you simply have no choice in the matter? But there were times that shit like that had to be sorted, especially when it was a friend's daughter, which had gotten herself caught up in the mess in the first place.

Fortunately, that only happened a couple of times through the years that I could remember, and usually when the boys found out that the girl was under age, they were quite eager to fix the situation, and make an even quicker retreat from it, typically distancing themselves, just as far away from the problem as they could get and just as fast.

After all, there are some things that you just don't do, even if you're an outlaw, and messing with little kids is definitely one of them.

By then, we had reached the motel/hotel that I was staying at and I simply said goodnight to the girl and then I handed her a twenty dollar bill just for good measure, because I knew that she'd be in a lot of trouble, if she went back empty handed to the guy in the restaurant. That's the way those chicken-hawks work, and I certainly didn't want her to get into any trouble, for any reason.

The girl smiled at me, thanked me for the note and then went cheerfully on her way, headed back to where we had just come from I'm sure, after all, Buddy the chicken hawk, was probably still sitting there and he'd be waiting for her, with his hands outstretched, along with his cold, dead eyes, no doubt. Anyway, it was none of my business and that was that as far as I was concerned.

I took the elevator up to the eighth floor, where I turned the key in the lock and then headed straight for the bed. I was way beyond being too tired to think about anything anymore and eventually I slept the entire night away, safe, sound and secure, except for those nightmares of course.

****

I was watching the television the following night, when a few soft knocks came to the door. It had been a few hours since I had gone outside, so I definitely wasn't expecting anyone and I wasn't sure who to expect anyway, but I had a gut feeling that it was going to be the girl again and that would only mean trouble for me.

Sure enough, I opened up the door and straight away I saw that she had been crying. I also saw the bruises on the side of her face and down her neck. One of her eyes was puffy from a fresh hit by the look of things.

A large red welt on her cheek bone, a blood shot eye and some clumped-up hair, which all in all, made her look as if she had just been put through some sort of wringer.

"Can you help me?" the girl said, as she entered the room and then quickly took a seat on the big ole easy chair that I had just got up from.

"I'm in trouble again and I really don't know what to do about it? I think he's actually gone crazy this time, because he just beat the hell out me in an alley-way for no reason at all, and so I ran. You were the only one that I could think about. So here I am."

"I told you the other night that this ain't any life for a kid, I quickly said, you should have listened to that and got yourself back home, where you belong."

"Home is just as bad, the girl said, my mother's boyfriend used to beat me up all the time as well, unless I gave him what he wanted, that is, which is why I ran away to begin with. He ain't nothing but a fucking pervert really and he drinks too much as well. I tried telling my mother that he was all over me when she wasn't around, but she wouldn't listen, so I left. I can't go back there anyway, it's been too long and I really don't know what else to do.

He's going to kill me if he finds me now. I was supposed to meet up with some of the guys that he knows, but I refused to do it, because they like to get it on, all at once, if you know what I mean and that always hurts me, in one way or another.

One of the guys likes to film it while they're doing it as well and he always tells the others what to do, like he's some kind of movie director or something.

They put a knife to my throat one night after they tied me to the bed. And then they brought in a chicken and made me watch as they chopped its head off and sprayed its blood all over me, and then they filmed me peeing myself, because I was so scared.

I swear he'd probably kill me if he could, because he's really a fucking asshole and he knows that I don't like him or the kind of things he does. He really scares the hell out me and the others just laugh about it. So my boyfriend started beating me up again, because I wouldn't do what they wanted me to do, in-fact, I don't want anything to do with them. They're just a bunch of sick people, doing some really sick things. I ran away from him as quick as I could and here I am. I'm really sorry about this; but I just don't know what else to do right now."

"What about calling the cops? I said, they'll help you out? They usually have places that young girl's can go. You know like women's shelters or Halfway houses, or something else? It has to be better than what you've got now."

"They just want to send me back home again she said, and I can't go back there, no way, no how. My mother's boyfriend just makes me want to puke and I know that I'll end up killing him somehow or he'll be killing me, one way or another. So, I can't do that, I just can't."

"Look girl, I said again, it has to be better than a life out on the streets. There are people that can deal with things like this; you just need to get them involved. If your mother's boyfriend is hurting you in anyway, tell them and let them deal with it. Because it beats getting beat on the street, if you know what I mean? You deserve better than that, in-fact, everyone does."

It was right about then, that the door came crashing in. Who would've thought?

****

I should've known that something was about to happen and I actually did, deep down inside, but I didn't know who, what or when for that matter.

Luckily, I was already standing at the time, talking to the girl as she was sitting there in the big ole easy chair that I had been sitting in, long before the she ever showed up.

I quickly glanced at the door, making a mental note of the noise and the various broken bits and pieces which were now lying on the carpet and I realized who the guy actually was, that was making his way through it, and then of course, I saw the gun that was held tightly in the guy's left hand.

All I can say after that; is that my basic instincts kicked in and I was all over the guy like a bloody hot rash that one might find on a child with measles.

I don't think he was expecting that, but he should have been, after all, if you're going to kick someone's door in, you better plan for the worst.

Anyway, the gun went off almost immediately during the initial scuffle, then it went off again and just as suddenly as it did, there was a great deal of pain in my right side. Two bloody tours of Nam under my belt at the time and now that I was back in the States, this asshole had just shot me, but that didn't stop me in the slightest, in-fact, it was almost the opposite.

I was fuming, as you would imagine, practically seeing red as they say, while being pumped full of adrenaline at the same time, then I was overwhelmed by a considerable amount of self-preservation, which to be honest, had always been there anyway, since I was four years old at least.

I wrestled with guy at first, knocking the gun out of his hand, before I slammed him up against the wall. I grabbed the top of his jacket and started swinging him around the room with it, punching him in the head a few times and kneeing him in groin, as I was doing it. I was still reeling from the pain, seeing red, black and just about every other colour that you could imagine, but of course, I didn't stop there.

I swung the guy around and punched him a few more times in the face for good measure and then just as the guy was starting to crumble, I let him go and for whatever reasons, I gave him one last kick to his chest. It was a side kick, up and out, but it was a little too much and definitely a little too late, for him anyway.

To be honest, it was a bit of blur after that, almost surreal. I was so angry at the time, that I couldn't think straight, but it was also a moment that was instantly filled with regret, a definitive moment, not just for me so much, but it certainly was for him, because suddenly, there was another loud noise, piercing the air in the room and shattered glass started flying everywhere.

The guy had flown through the bloody window, which was definitely not what I had planned, nor what I had even wanted to do at the time, but it was too late to take it back now, it was already done and dusted and there was no changing that.

He didn't even have a chance to scream. He just fell through the window, eight floors down and head first straight into a dumpster that had been left there for the garbage. Dead in the middle of a garbage can, wow, how appropriate, I thought, as I looked down on him.

The dumpster was empty, except for one piece of trash, which had been dropped, pretty much dead in the middle of it, along with the shards of glass from the window that fell down right along with him.

Now I can tell you that there's a lot of things that run through your mind pretty damn quick, when you kill someone. Most of the time, you might have a good reason for it or you're under orders from someone else, as I had been in the past, but mainly, it's just business as usual and you barely give it a second thought, but this time, well this time it was a little different.

It wasn't much more than an accident really; self-defence at the worst, or perhaps manslaughter, if anyone had cared to push it hard enough. Although I'm quite sure that, that piece of shit deserved every little bit of it, and I certainly wasn't crying over it, that's for sure. After all, it was him or me, and that guy was just another low-life, POS scumbag anyway, as far as I was concerned, that had finally left the planet with a little help of course, but the girl was hysterical by then; she didn't know what to do, how to act, what to say, or where to go for that matter.

I actually had to slap her, just to get her to calm down. Then I did my best to keep her calm for the next few minutes by telling her not to worry about anything, that it hadn't really happened and that no-one would ever know about it anyway, because I'd get it all cleaned up, before anyone even suspected that the guy was even gone. Then I handed her a few hundred bucks that I had stashed in my wallet which she immediately took of course, without any hesitation, I might add.

"Look I said, I just did you a favour and if I were you, I'd take that money and get yourself on a bus heading out of town, real quick like. Head on back home and deal with that asshole boyfriend of your mothers if you have to, and forget about everything else that's happened here tonight, because it never really happened as far as you're concerned and you were never really here to begin with. It was just a crazy dream or a vivid nightmare at the most and it never happened anyway.

It really is as simple as that, trust me Ok? I'll give you a number to call, if you have any more problems, all you have to do is tell them that I gave it to you in the first place. They're some pretty good friends of mine and they understand about these sorts of things. If you can't straighten out your home life because of your mother's boyfriend, then call the number and they'll be happy to help you out, you have my word on that. Apart from that, just forget that you ever met me and you'll be fine, ok? So go on now, get the hell out of here and don't come back."

"I'm scared, the girl said, he has a lot of friends out there and if they ever find out that he's been killed, then they'll be looking for me, and I don't want that, that's for sure."

"Look I said again, just let me handle this, I'll take you down to the bus station and see you off. No-one will ever know where you went, I promise you that and they won't be able to track you down, no matter what, even if they wanted to.

If they ever did, you'll have that number to call and trust me; my friends are a whole lot different to any scum bags that this guy could have ever known.

Once you're out of here, don't come back, it's as simple as that. That piece of shit has just taken a walk and disappeared, that's all. He's done a runner, like they all do eventually, he's simply gone and that's that. His so-called friends will think that he took off with their money anyway.

He'll never be back and he'll never bother you or anyone else again. So just go back home and forget about it, alright?"

She wanted to argue with me some more, but I didn't have the time for that, so I took her by the arm and headed out the door, down the hall to the elevator and finally into the street just as fast as the elevator took to get us down to the ground.

I had already seen that there was another dumpster sitting next to the dumpster that this piece of shit had dropped in, which I also noticed was partially full of used garbage bags. So I quickly tossed several of those bags over to the other one and then I used them to cover up the dead guy's body.

Yeah, I actually checked to make sure that the guy was dead first of course, but that was only too fucking obvious. There was blood and brain matter, all over the place. His eyes were open and he had a stupid look on his face, but one of his collar bones was sticking out from the wrong side of his neck and there wasn't any blood coming from the open wound, so yeah, he was dead alright. Dead as dead can get.

Once I did that, I went ahead and took the girl down to the bus station on the back of my clubs motorcycle. I also made sure that we weren't being followed by any of the guys that the girl might have been worried about. I took us down different streets and I even circled around the block a few times, before I finally pulled into the bus station. Then I waited around for the girl's bus to come in and made damn sure that she was on it just as quickly as she could be, which was about thirty minutes later and hopefully with no-one any wiser.

I had already made some calls by then, while we were both waiting around for the bus to leave, even though it was early hours of the morning. I needed some help and of course, I knew exactly who to call for that as usual.

Now, I could have called the spring's club, but this wasn't their problem to begin with, and Uncle Sam never sleeps anyway, so by eight am, the door and the window had been fixed, the mess had been cleaned up and the garbage had been taken away. Perfect, I thought; out of sight and out of mind, now for some much needed rest.

Of course, the brass wanted to end my furlough right then and there, something about mixing a military jurisdiction with a civilian authority and all that, but I managed to talk them out of that, after all, I only had a couple days left of my leave anyway and I really did want to rest up.

No-one paid attention to the shots that rang out that night or the broken glass that was still laying on the ground after the bin was taken away, or even the fact that people were coming and going long before the sun came up.

If they had seen or even heard any of it to begin with, they certainly didn't say anything about it, but then there's no surprise there; because cities are like that, especially a city at night, because no-one really cares about what goes on to begin with, unless it affects them personally that is.

The second bullet had hit me in the side, but luckily, it had simply bounced off my hip bone and then crumpled itself onto the inside of the outside wall.

It was eventually found during the clean-up of course, along with the 38 snub-nosed revolver that it came from in the first place. An old Saturday night special, as they called it at the time. And not knowing what crimes had been committed with it, we all made damn sure that it disappeared with the dead guy in the end as well. I certainly didn't want that coming back to haunt me, or anyone else, for that matter. The first shot, had gone straight through the bottom of the window, leaving a small hole and structural damage to the glass, which is why the guy went through it so easy in the first place? Was that coincidence, or simply Providence? Who could really say? Maybe it was just his time to go?

A day later and I had rested up enough. It was time to move on, after all, I had things to do, people to see and places to go to etc. And I was finally starting to feel a little more normal again, re-charged, perhaps even ready for business as usual.

The girl called the number I gave to her eventually, telling the guy who answered the phone, to thank me for what I did and she also said, that she had finally worked things out with her mother and that they had both moved down to Florida, without any boyfriends in tow, and if I was ever down that way, to be sure to look her up. I never heard from her again after that, although Florida was one of my tri-yearly stops for the longest time, which was a good thing really, no matter which way you look at it? I always figured that she had gotten on with whatever she had to do with her life and I wished her well for that. I could only hope that she had finally met herself a nice guy and had settled down eventually, but you never know, because life always has a way of repeating itself, even at the best of times.

I got promoted again after that, who would've thought? And then I finally got stationed where I had actually wanted to be stationed all along, which of course, was almost perfect for me and the club, for a while anyway, but that's just another story that I'll get into later.

****

Now it's funny sometimes, how life works out. You think that you have some kind of control over it, at least most of the time, but then you find out that you don't and you never did. Especially if you're involved with any type of corporate machine, whether it's the military or not, because they always do exactly what they want to do, and you have to comply, whether you want to or not. And even if you think it's all your idea to begin with, you eventually find out that it's nowhere near and it never has been. Sometimes, it even seems like there's a guiding force, that's been pushing you along the way, whether you wanted it or not?

Perhaps it's fate, kismet, destiny, or maybe it's just plain ole luck? I don't know, but it's always there just the same and I find myself questioning the reasons behind it all, because I know inside that it can't all be coincidental, even though others may have gone through the exact same things.

******

Postscript

Years later, I read an article in one of the newspapers, about a state Senator who had just gotten married, and had his wedding ceremony down in the Florida Keys.

The article was filled with pertinent information; probably more than what should have been there in the first place and there were pictures of the wedding, along with most of their guests. I won't tell you their names, but it was quite literally an affair of the century. It was A Triple-A listing, all the way around, rich, lavish, elegant and highly sophisticated.

Of course the bride was strikingly beautiful, in-fact she was a drop-dead gorgeous type of woman, in more ways than one. She had grown into an elegant, strong, and almost dazzling kind of woman through the years. She held her head high, she smiled a lot and people were simply awed by her presence.

You could see straight away that she had definitely come up in the world on the right side of life, no-matter what was thrown at her. I was happy about that, after all, it was a long ways away from that night in Denver and I knew that she had made all the right choices after all.

****

17
Another Trip to the Past

"Bloody rain" I said, walking out of the doors of the casino that night, watching several transparent little droplets, splash off the top of the tank and then run down to where they gradually pooled, at the indented part of the saddle, which was still firmly attached to the motorcycle, that was strategically parked-up in a slightly perpendicular manner, not quite in an up-right position, with its short ass-end, hard-up against the concrete curb.

The bike itself was drenched, and it was only too obvious that I was about to be as well. Who would've thought?

It's been the worst weather all year I thought, as I straddled that long, lean, low machine and then quickly sat down in what was left of that puddle, after I had previously swiped it clear, with the back of my already gloved hand. At the same time, I impatiently hit the start-up button, and listened carefully as the motor coughed a little, watching, as it puffed out a small cloud of bluish/white smoke, just before it finally roared into life and then started to rumble, like only a large V-Twin motor can. It was pretty obvious that it didn't like the weather much neither.

"If I had wanted wet," I yelled out loud, looking upwards towards the heavens as I said it. "I would have bought a bloody Jet ski, instead of a damn motorcycle." And then I laughed a little, as I noticed that the doorman had over heard me. He was smiling, and shaking his head.

"Well, it's true" I said, smiling back at him, figuring that the guy probably thought that I was either drunk, or just plain crazy, which was the usual kind of response I'd get from most of the citizens around my neck of the woods, even the bouncer types, at times. But hey, this wasn't my neck of the woods at the moment, and I really didn't know what to expect?

So, I squeezed the clutch, kicked the stand, cranked the throttle and in less than a blink of your grannies eye, I roared off into the middle of the night, like a madman on some kind of mission, out there doing his thing as usual.

I didn't really mind the rain though, in-fact, I was quite used to it by then, living back in Britain as I did at the time. Typically, it kept me feeling a little more awake and perhaps even more alert than what I usually was.

Sometimes, it even kept me feeling more alive than what I thought I should have been, not that I didn't feel alive most of the time anyway, because I really did and you can bet that I was pretty grateful for that.

It's just that when I rode my bike, there was nothing else in the world that could truly beat that feeling, except for maybe having sex of course, but I usually liked that fairly slow, smooth and easy most of the time, not really fast and furious like I was known to ride.

Oh sure, I'd get down and dirty when I had to, and trust me, I had even wanted to at times, but not that often. I was more of a let it come to me type of guy, rather than the go out and get it type, and tonight was simply made for riding anyway. In-fact to me, if the truth were known, every night was made for riding, because that's what I've always lived for and that's what I've always done.

What a night though, I thought, as I scooted along those dark, damp and empty streets, noticing just how cold and lonely they actually felt, especially for that time of year and for that time of the morning. Not a soul in sight back then, but never mind, it was the eighties and there was only half the population of what it is today.

My first stop of the night had been Soho, deep in the heart of the big ole smoke that never sleeps. It was a favourite little hang-out of mine, along with a few others that I knew, not too far from the clubhouse and just up the road from where I was staying.

Then it was due east to South-end on Sea, for a roll of the dice and to drop some coins in a machine. And finally, it was all the way down south to the Brighton coast, of all places. Not exactly the greatest road trip in the world, I might add, but hey, it was definitely all right, for a Saturday night.

My custom chopper had sweetly purred all the way along, as I quickly guided it around every corner and bend that was out there at the time. It was the prettiest machine, that's ever been seen. It was long, it was lean, it was mean and it was green. Who would've thought?

Yeah, that's right it was green. Actually, it was a shit kind of Green and I've always hated that colour, ever since my army days, in-fact, I swore that if I ever had to see that colour again, it'd be too damn soon, but sure enough, green is what I got, or more to the point, it was an olive-drab type of green, a really shit kind of green when you think about it, and of course, I had to think about it all the time now.

To begin with, I had wanted it two-tone, or perhaps even a flip colour, which was known as Tonic, back in the day. You probably know exactly what I mean? Blue, grey, silver, or perhaps even black, depending on how the light hits it and the angle that you saw it at. I even thought about different shades of purple for awhile, which would have been too damn pretty in the long run, but instead of taking it to the man who could paint it up that way, I decided to do it myself, to save a little time and money etc, and sure enough, as luck would have it, it came out green and man was it ever green.

Never mind, it really didn't matter what colour it was in the grand scheme of things, because it was still the best damn ride around and it was all mine. All mine, along with a grubby little bank manager, who thought that I was the scum of the earth that is, and the club that I was involved with of course, but that's just another story that'll have to wait.

Soho was kicking as usual. It's one of "The" places to go, if you want to party hard in London, at any time of the day or night, because the clubs stay open until the early hours of the morning and they're always full of Wine, Whiskey, Women, and Song, or anything else that your heart desires, and most of them are simply "waiting for the taking" as they usually say, just as long as you've got the cash to splash and the time to shine, that is.

It was one of those "Women," that had actually started me out on this little road trip, in the first place. She was a tall, slender, well-built, dark-haired, little beauty, with big green, bedroom eyes, that could've easily sucked any red-blooded man, or woman, right into the centre of them, whether they wanted it or not, and when I first drew my own eyes on her, I was lost to them and I couldn't keep myself from looking at her, not for a single minute, right from the get go.

The girl also had a gorgeous set of legs that wouldn't quit. They were long, thin and shapely, wrapped-up tight in a pair of faded blue and grey, denim fashioned jeans that all the girls seemed to be wearing back then, which of course, got a little bit cheeky at the top, in a good way that is. At least that's what I thought anyway.

Needless to say, she was a woman, that had a fine looking ass on her and her hair was simply to die for as well. It too, was long, soft, and flowing, dark, silky and mysterious, you know the kind of woman that I'm talking about, and yes, you could say that she looked a lot like an Angel, but the reality of it all was that she had the Devil wrapped-up inside of her and he was itching to get out, just as quick as he possibly could.

I'd seen it all before of course, so it was nothing special to me. Good looking women are a dime a dozen they say, and most of the time, they really aren't worth the hassle that you know they'll end up putting you through, especially in the long run, but for some reason, I believed that this one, might just be, a little different.

Now most guys would have loved the way that this woman looked and I'd be the first to admit that. After all, I wasn't any different myself; I've always had an eye for a beautiful woman, what can I say? But I wasn't looking for anything special that night or any other night to be quite honest. After all, I was already committed to the club and I was living that life to the Hilt.

I used to get my loving on the run, simply because I stayed on the road most of the time. I was more than just a little happy with that, after all, that was my life back then and that's the way it had always been.

Still, we immediately struck up a conversation that seemed to go on forever, and it didn't really matter what was said, I'd just laugh, and the woman would laugh and then I'd keep on saying it or something else just as funny, or just as stupid? You know how conversations are?

To be honest, this woman reminded me of someone that I had known when I was younger, someone that I had met back in my late teenage years, when I was still in the army, during my airborne/recon training days, across the pond, somewhere in North Carolina, probably?

North Carolina is a beautiful state, although Fort Bragg, and the Special Forces, which were known as the Green Berets, at that time, had a lot to be desired, but never mind, it was only one of several bases, that I had trained at over time, and they were all pretty much the same.

Nothing ever happened from that meeting though, the girl was way too young and besides that, I moved around too much. We came from different backgrounds, knew different people, and moved in different circles.

We were the opposite types of people if the truth were known, and I guess that I knew that, even back then, because I was never going to be the suit and tie kind of guy that her father was, and the girl was never going to be a world traveller, or even a biker for that matter, but I'll never forget the way that I felt about her at the time and I often wondered, if she had ever thought about me?

I guess everyone has a memory like that, stashed away somewhere at the back of their mind. What could've, would've, should've been, but of course it never was.

Anyway, within an hour or so, this woman figured that she had me wrapped up tight, right around her little finger, for the night anyway, and to tell you the truth, I was pretty happy that she had, because to me, she was a beauty that's for sure, a drop-dead gorgeous type of female, in every aspect of the way and then some.

I was younger back then as well, wild, single and carefree, but I still had my values and my wits about me. This woman was one of the best looking women, that I had ever laid eyes on at the time and I figured that if I played my cards right, maybe we could make some sort of sweet music together, after all she was raising my blood pressure, that's for sure, and I was aching to get to know her better, to say the least. I was also hoping that the girl was feeling the same way about me.

Now you'd probably have to give her some credit though; because, she had pulled out every trick in the book that she could think of when she first saw me.

She batted both of her sexy eyes and gave me one of the broadest of smiles, that you've ever seen at the time, and she constantly licked her lips, as we stood there talking. She also played the Damsel in distress a few times, getting caught-up on something at the bar, and then once again at the bathroom door. She even slipped over in front of me, so that I actually had to catch her, before she fell to the floor and she was good at sending out all kinds of other body language as well that just didn't seem to quit.

She danced like a professional dancer, grinding herself into me, fast and furious at times and then really slow and easy, at other times.

It was hard for me to concentrate on anything else; I was completely lost in the moment, and I was definitely lost in her.

Then we kissed, and it actually felt as though I'd lose my front teeth, even though they were still firmly attached and all of this happened within the first hour or so of meeting her.

Man, I was feeling like a lucky guy. I was so excited by her, in so many different ways. She made every man's head in the club turn sideways when they saw her, and then she made damn sure that they all knew that she was with me.

Yeah, she was special all right, young, beautiful, elegant, a little sophisticated, and she was all mine, for the night anyway.

It was her idea to go to South-end on Sea to begin with, who would've thought?

Of course, she had never been on the back of a motorcycle before, the poor little sheltered thing, that she claimed to be, and I was only too eager, to make her first time out, simply one of the best times, that she'd ever have.

So it didn't take any persuasion at all, to get us both out of the club that night and on to the highway. We practically floated out the door, arm in arm, and then we flew on down the road, like a couple of love birds, looking for an empty nest.

The woman wrapped herself up so tight around me, that it felt like I was wearing an extra jacket at the time, which was a pretty good feeling; I'd happily admit, because the long night air was cool, crisp and clean, without a single drop of rain in sight, I might add.

The throttle was cranked-up, as we listened to the motor purr. It was one of the best sounds in the world, well almost the best sound anyway.

We both enjoyed the night-time ride and when it was over, which is always too soon as far as I was concerned; we were both inside a casino, throwing dice on a cloth covered table, with a lot of signs and numbers on it.

Which was her idea again, of course, having never been to a casino before, at least not in South-end on Sea? And it was just lucky, that I had been paid for a job that I'd just finished the day before, and that I actually had some extra cash to spare that evening, because none of it was cheap that's for sure, but then again, gambling, wine and women, never are.

We quickly moved on to the roulette tables, and then over to the card tables, before we finally hit a few slot machines.

She laughed, I laughed, and we had what seemed to be one of the greatest times of all. It was almost like; we belonged together, like we were even made for each other, hell, it even felt like we were out on our honeymoon at one point in time, or at least something similar.

Everyone noticed us of course, and they especially noticed her, who was simply, the most gorgeous woman that I had ever met at the time.

We were known as the Beauty and the Biker, which was a statement that I overheard the bartender saying as he sorted out our drinks.

"I know, she suddenly said out loud, with a huge smile on her face, just as I lost another twenty-quid, on three reels out of five, that didn't quite line up right, let's go to Brighton."

"Brighton I said, what the hell's going on down in Brighton, of all places?"

"I've got some people down there, she said again, we can spend the night with them and in the morning we can jump into the ocean. You do know how to swim don't you?"

I just laughed and then I said, "We live on an Island don't we love? Of course I know how to swim. Besides that, I spent the first nine months of my fucking life, stuck in a pool of bloody water."

"Good, she replied, laughing at the joke, because you'd be surprised how many people around here don't know how to swim. In-fact, some people have never even been to the ocean before, how sad is that?"

"That's because we live in the North Atlantic, I replied again, and the water around here is too damn cold, even in the summer time. If we lived in the South Pacific, then everyone would know how to swim" I said, looking back at her with a broad smile.

"What are you, some sort of Geography Teacher now?" The girl asked, laughing again and again, and then she said, "Come on then, let's go to Brighton, it'll be fun."

"Oh, ok I finally said, we'll get out of here."

So off we went for another two and half hour ride, back to the west from where we had already been and then all the way down south to the Brighton sea front, just as fast as the roads would take us.

I wasn't stopping for man or beast, I was on a mission now, and that was all there was to that. It was all done underneath a cool, twilight sky and by the time we got to Brighton, I was a little tired, the woman was a little stiff, we were both a little cold and we both needed to pee. We were also thirsty as hell, a little bit hungry and ready for another smoke.

The pubs were already closed by then, but most of the clubs were still open and the casinos were open twenty-four hours a day anyway, if you knew which ones to go to, that is?

We had several choices of where to go to next, though, and always being amiable, I let her decide, and she chose an out of the way casino, which was down along the sea front, not too far from the pier.

For the next few hours, we danced and drank the night away, laughing, kissing, hugging, and more, basically having a great time in general, but again this little trip was getting pretty damn expensive.

One night out on the town with this woman, had already set me back a week's wages or more, and I was almost out of cash by then, thinking about finding a hole-in-the-wall somewhere, to tap into my savings, which I really didn't want to do.

"What about your friends?" I finally asked her at last, just as the music was starting to wind down a bit and the crowd was thinning out on the dance floor.

"Where do they live and which way do we go to get there from here?"

"Oh, she said, I couldn't get a hold of them, so I just figured that we'd get a hotel room for the night and then try to find them tomorrow, after we go for a swim of course."

Finally, I thought, we'll get a room together, go to bed, have some fun and in the morning maybe even order up some room service. But for whatever reasons and who knows why, I opened up my mouth, and then I stuck my foot, straight into it.

I started saying all the wrong things, at all the wrong times, for all the wrong bloody reasons. I knew what I was saying of course, but it really didn't matter. I just kept on talking, saying all the things that I shouldn't have, when I should have just stopped and kicked myself in the teeth instead, but I didn't. Of course I didn't. Who would've thought?

"Cool babe, I said, I hope that you have some money for all that then, because I'm starting to get a little skint right now, especially after all of this partying tonight and I only just got paid yesterday."

"You're joking, right? The woman said, rather quick and harsh, and without that pretty smile of hers, I might add.

Don't you have enough money left, for a hotel room? It's only for the night and I'm sure that it won't cost anymore than a couple of hundred quid or so, after all, this is Brighton. Come on now; don't be messing around with me like that."

I don't know what it was really, maybe I was just too tired to deal with it, or maybe it was something else, but I certainly didn't like the way that she said what she had just said. Besides that, it didn't sound very nice. In-fact, it sounded more like a spoilt child, chastising her parents for getting her the wrong bloody doll as a birthday gift, and I could never stand spoilt kids to begin with, I never have and I never would. What more could you say about that?

I turned to her and said, "Well, actually, no my love, I don't have the money any more, shaking my head at the same time, we've blown over a thousand quid tonight, what with all the casinos and all of the drinks that we've had. So, I guess, we'll just have to go home from here then, your place or mine, it doesn't really matter to me which one it is."

"What?" The woman said again, with a voice that was loud enough for all of the others to hear, I can't go home now; my old man would kill me, and besides that, I wasn't supposed to be out tonight, let alone, out with the likes of you."

"What? I said back at her, in total and utter disbelief, Wait a minute; you're telling me now, that you're married? I thought you already told me that you were single?"

"Yeah right, she said, we're all bloody single. I just happen to have somebody waiting for me at home that's all, and don't start thinking that I'm going home with you neither, because I'm not. I'm definitely not that kind of girl."

I was floored by then, because we had already been together just like that, all night long. Laughing, kissing, hugging, and practically having sex on the bloody dance floor.

The woman had even let her hand drop to my manhood, more than just a few times, during the course of the evening, that's for sure, and I was simply aching to get her into bed; pull her knickers off, slip in-between her legs, then slide my tongue around her little button and deep inside her honey pot, making her scream a little, before I inserted myself and finally exploded in some much needed relief, but now she was saying that she's not that kind of girl? What the fuck is that about?

"What's your problem? I said to her again, in complete, and utter, disbelief? You sure have been acting like that kind of girl, at least for the last six or seven hours now, or more. Are you crazy or what?"

"Screw you biker trash, she said, as she stepped away from me. Screw you and piss right off. I never want to see you again. You're just another greased-up, useless little wanker, that doesn't have a fucking clue, about anything at all, really."

I was completely stunned by then. It was the first time that I had heard the woman swear.

What a waste of space, I thought and what a damn fool I'd been to spend all that money trying to impress her like I had. Shit! Fuck, damn it all to hell.

Oh well, screw her too, it was time for me to scoot on out of there anyway. So, that's when I left her.

The woman just stood there of course, with a drink in her hand which I had already paid for, a horrible scorn on her face, and some pretty sharp and nasty words that were rolling off the tip of her tongue.

She didn't look so appealing to me now though I thought, as I headed out the door, trying to remember where it was that I had parked-up my bike at. Shame really, I bet she would have been pretty lame in bed as well, I thought again, laughing to myself.

****

Anyway, that's about where we came in with this story to begin with, because that's when the skies opened up, and the rain started to fall, and boy, did it ever come down hard.

Now the rain can be just about as miserable as the weather can get for a biker, unless it turns to into snow and ice that is. It stings you when it hits you in the face, it makes the roads, wet and slippery, and it makes your clothes, feel cold, damp, and sticky, whether they are or not, and then your mind simply goes numb, faster than you can count the minutes ticking by, and that's just on a good day.

Even when the rain isn't falling yet, you can still feel it in the air, and you can taste it at the back of your throat, and let me tell you, it was definitely raining by the time that I had left that crazy woman in the club that night. In-fact, it was more than a little rain; it was torrential and it was coming down in sheets, by the bucketful.

Never mind, I thought as I headed back out through the city, and then straight onto the highway that would eventually lead me up north, towards where I was living at the time.

I figured that it would only take me a good hour and a half or so to get back home, if I hurried, but then again, only if it stopped raining.

Fortunately, by the time I got to the edge of town the rain was easing up. In-fact, by then it was a light rain falling, for the moment anyway, so I was able to get a scoot on, taking the bike up to speed in no time at all.

It wasn't long before I noticed that I was somewhere just south of some services, when the heavens started to open up again. It was another mad downpour, which saw more sheets of water, blowing wildly across the open road.

The wind had come up as well, slowing me and the rest of the traffic down to little more than just a crawl that time, so I pulled off the highway at the main entrance to the services, just as quickly as I could and just in time to hear my headlight pop.

"Shit, I said out loud, well that's just frickin perfect, now I'll be stuck here until daylight." It was already past four in the morning, so I knew that I wouldn't have to wait too long for daylight. Another hour or so and it would be plenty light enough.

I probably had a bulb kicking around somewhere as well, and besides that I was hungry at the time. So, I parked-up at the curb as usual, shook myself off, and then I quickly went inside the restaurant.

Of course, everyone in there stared at me for a minute or two, as I slowly walked passed them un-zipping my jacket at the same time, but they quickly looked the other way, as soon as I caught their eyes in mine.

You could easily see that I wasn't the only traveller on the road that morning; because there were lots of them really, but no bikers at all, except for me of course, and I guess it was kind of typical of regular citizens anyway; because they can't help staring at a biker, even though they usually don't have the balls to look one straight in the eyes.

Never mind though, I probably did look like an overgrown rat at that moment in time anyway. Perhaps one that had just swam its way up from the sewer no doubt. So, I took off my jacket as soon as I could and then I hung it over the end of the booth, with my colours, tags, and rockers, completely visible for all to see. Then I sat down and ordered up a cup of coffee just as quickly as I could.

I didn't want people thinking that I was out to rob the place, or something, if you know what I mean?

The waitress was a pretty little thing, young, well dressed, with a good looking build on her and a warm, soft, gorgeous smile, along with an even warmer greeting that I appreciated at the time.

She was short, blonde, fairly thin, and all of about twenty-one or so, I figured. She also had some nice words to go along with her good looks as well, as I soon found out, sitting there, drinking my first cup of coffee, and slowly trying to dry out.

"A bit wet out there, isn't it sweetie? The waitress said, still smiling. Have you been out there for very long?"

"I just rode up from Brighton, I said, smiling back at her, and I'm slowly making my way back home to London now."

"Where's that then?" The waitress said again, still smiling and checking out all of the patches that I had on my jacket at the same time, as well as eyeing up the length of my pony tail?

"Brighton I said with a really big grin, or London?" Then I sipped on some more coffee, watching her, as she looked me up and down.

"I actually live in Brixton," I said to her again. The waitress smiled some more, looking at me, and then she said.

"Oh yeah, Brixton, looking down at my jacket again, of course you do. It seems like everyone's from London these days, so what's going down in Brighton then?" she asked, just as another customer came in and sat down at the counter. I was about to tell her, when she said,

"Listen hon. I'll be back in a minute, do you want anything else? I could always bring you some breakfast, if you like?"

"Yes please, I said, I'd like the full English breakfast if I may, with toast and strawberry jam on the side, thank you."

I watched her walk away. She was a nice girl, I thought, as I stared out the window, watching sheets of water, still blowing across the parking lot. In-fact, she was probably a real warm and genuine type of person, who was into much slower time's maybe, like sipping wine in front of an open fire, with light scented candles burning over the top of a wooden mantel piece, somewhere soft, safe, warm and secure.

She was probably, nothing like the woman that I had gotten hooked up with earlier on. That one was the down and dirty type for sure, a crazy, frigging nut job that I should never have been bothered with in the first place.

After all, I knew better? I wasn't a bad looking guy at all; tall, dark, and ruggedly handsome, as some people would say, and I had a great sense of humour, most of the time. But that woman, that woman was just too damn good to be true, right from the get-go, too good for me, that's for sure; at least that's what she thought anyway.

Oh well, it was a good job that I got rid of her when I did, because it definitely wouldn't have worked out for either one of us in the long run, after all, we were way too different, and beside that, I wasn't out for anything long term anyway.

She might have been a good looking woman alright, but like my old man always use to say, "if you can't trust em son, then you're better off without them, because they'll get you into a world of trouble quicker than shit otherwise, and you wouldn't want that for anyone, not even your worst enemy."

What a freaking nightmare though. Good riddance to bad rubbish and all of that. Still, I had better things to do with my time.

Right about then, my eyes caught sight of a Red Ferrari, just as it pulled into the parking lot and then parked itself, up next to my chopper.

It was a nice looking car, I thought, although the colour was a bit too bright for my taste, but at least it wasn't green, you'd have to give him credit for that.

Then, before I even realized what was happening, I saw this leggy, dark-haired beauty; quickly get out of the passenger seat and make a mad dash for the restaurants door. She didn't even wait for the driver.

Holy shit, I thought again, as I realized what was going on. It was her of all people. She must have gotten her old man to come down and get her, or perhaps this was the friend that she couldn't get hold of earlier?

There was nothing that I could do about it though, the woman had already seen my motorcycle as soon as they pulled into the parking lot, so I just sat there watching her, as she stormed into the restaurant like she owned the place, of course, glaring at all of the people that were still sitting there, and then finally, she focused her cold, heartless stare, on yours truly and she didn't even blink, not even once.

"Don't you even talk to me, you bastard," she said, just about as loud as she could, almost stomping over to the table, where she then, just flopped herself down, right in front of me.

"I can't believe that you dumped me like that, you little prick and in Brighton of all places. Do you realize that I could have been killed or maybe robbed and beaten, or even raped? Maybe, something far worse than that could have happened to me as well and it's all because of you, you leather bound, brainless, little maggot."

I was still watching the Ferrari outside, trying really hard to ignore her, although it wasn't working out too well, because she was starting to sound like my mother and I couldn't stand her, but anyway I could also see this huge, mountain of a man, with arms the size of tree trunks and a neck about the size of both of my upper legs put together, slowly crawl out of the driver's seat.

I kid you not, this guy could have been the incredible Hulks little brother for all I knew. He was built like a brick shithouse and I could only imagine that the rest of his family, were probably built the exact same way, even his mother.

I just sat there and watched as the guy shut the car door, and then rapidly made his way to the entrance. I was just about to say something like, well; it really was your idea to begin with woman, when this big ole boy, quickly lumbered on over to the table as well.

"Do you know this guy then?" the big guy said, with a fairly deep voice, looking down at both of us, but looking at me in particular, with a long, cold, hard, angry, type of stare. Not quite the friendly little giant that he should've been, I thought, especially so early in the morning.

"Chill out man, I said, just as the guy was about to say something else. I didn't know that she was married and as soon as I found out about it, I split, all right? I ain't looking for any trouble here; I've got enough of that on my plate as it is."

"She's married? The big guy said, almost fuming by then, well, man oh man, that just about takes the piss now, don't it?

She told me, that her "boyfriend" had dumped her off at the club and that her sister was waiting for her to get back home, so that she could watch her kids, before they headed off to school."

I could see that the guy was eyeing up my jacket now, which was still hanging on the backside of the booth drying out, where I had originally put it when I took it off.

His voice was starting to trail off; rather quickly, I might add, as he realized who it was that he was actually talking to.

I was also thinking, that it's Sunday you fool, although, I didn't say anything, because there wasn't any reason to upset the guy, anymore than he already was.

I just figured that I needed to keep him calm really, because at the end of the day, it wasn't his fault that we were all sitting there. I'd jump up and break his nose in a heartbeat if I had to, and then I'd probably take him out at the knees, quicker than he could imagine or even think about, but only if he kicked off first. After all, I didn't know him from Adam, so I had no reason to get into it with him, unless he was the one to push it of course.

Then the woman started up again, and the whole damned restaurant seemed to perk-up.

"Ah for fucks sakes, the woman started screaming, now look what you've done, you fucking loser. This guy, is one of the owners of that club, that you left me stranded at, you dumb-assed moron; he's giving me a ride home and you're going to fuck the whole thing up."And then to everyone's surprise and just as quick the big guy turned to her and said, "You've got to be joking honey, I'm not giving you a ride home now, that's for sure. You can find your own way home from here and by the way, I never said that I owned that place neither, I just work there, but that doesn't matter anymore, because I don't need any of this shit in my life, especially with someone like you."

Then he turned to me again and quickly said, "I sure hope I didn't get myself into any kind of problem here, friend. I was just trying to help her out really, that's all it was. I certainly don't want any trouble coming from it, especially your kind of trouble."

I could see the big guy was looking a little worried by then, his eyebrows were starting to sweat, he had a waver in his voice and I swear that he was even starting to shake a little, as if he had just come out of a bathtub full of ice.

Then I watched, as he quickly turned around, and walked right back towards the door that he had just come in from.

"C ya," he said again, as he headed back outside, without a second thought.

The woman and I, along with the rest of the people in the restaurant, just sat there watching in silence, as the big ole guy practically tore open the door of his own car, and then quickly squeezed himself back into the driver's seat, before he finally pulled away, splashing water all over the parking lot and the not so pretty green chopper that was still sitting out there, practically drowning in all of that pouring rain. Yeah, that's right, my green chopper, of course.

"Oh yeah, that's fucking great, the woman finally said, practically yelling at me again, how many more times are you going to screw up my life tonight, you idiot, wanker, greaser, loser, biker scum."

The waitress came over right about then, and then she asked me if everything was all right? Then she told the pair of us, to keep the noise level down because everyone in the whole place was listening in.

I agreed with her and then I immediately apologized, before turning my eyes back to the dark-haired woman, who was still sitting there, with me.

"Look woman, I said, it's not my fault that you're screwing around on your old man and as far as I'm concerned, you probably deserve what you get, but don't be yelling at me about it, because it was all your idea to begin with. You're just lucky that I'm a gentleman, otherwise I would've nailed your little ass to the wall by now, if I wasn't."

"Gentleman, she said, in a slightly lower tone of voice, but still high enough for everyone else to hear. You're no fucking gentleman, you're just a screwed up biker, without a pot to piss in. I know what you are and I've known plenty of fools, just like you. I also know that you really want me, because you can't take your eyes off of me, but you can't afford me neither, so keep your damn mouth shut, and leave me the fuck alone, you useless, no good maggot, go on, piss off."

I looked at her again, shaking my head, smiling as broadly as I could and quickly thinking that at least we finally agreed on something. She definitely was high maintenance, that's for sure, and then I laughed out loud and said, "Hey bitch, this is my table, so if you don't like it, then you can be the one to piss off. Go on now, find your own table, or better yet, just get the hell out of here altogether, because I was here first, and I haven't finished my fucking breakfast yet."

The woman started to say something else, but then she just burst into tears instead. "I'm sorry, she said, I really do like you. I was just having some fun tonight, that's all, my old man beats me up all the time and."

"Lookee here woman, I quickly said, cutting her off in the middle of her sentence. I don't want to hear this shit. If you get beat up by your husband, then you probably deserve it. If you don't like it, get a fucking divorce like everyone else does, and quit screwing with people's heads, especially mine.

If you hadn't lied to me in the first place, neither one of us would even be sitting here right now, so it's your own damn fault, not mine."

"All right, all right, she said, smiling back at me now, I get your point, and I'm really sorry, I truly am, I just needed that ride home and now I wish we hadn't stopped here in the first place, but we did.

Then, right out of the blue, she said, "Do you think that you could you buy me a cup of coffee please, and maybe a bite to eat as well, because I didn't realize how hungry I am. Please?"

I looked at her for a moment or two; she really was a beautiful woman. Too bad she was so screwed-up in the head.

Too bad she was married and too bad it was still raining, because otherwise, I would have just got up and left the place, leaving her right along with it, but instead I called the waitress back over and asked her nicely to bring the woman a cup of coffee, and a breakfast sandwich, as well as another cup of coffee for myself. After that, we just sat there looking at each other in complete and total silence for quite some time.

The waitress had already brought my breakfast to the table, earlier on and I was digging into it, enjoying the country sausage, mixed in with the strawberry jam that I had put on my toast as usual. But then I got to thinking again, this woman still looked pretty familiar to me and that had been bugging me all night long, although I couldn't quite place where it was that I'd seen her before, or even if I really had seen her before?

There was feeling though, a feeling that we had known each other briefly, at some point in time, but then someone put Trace Walton's "Black Hearted Woman" on the jukebox and it started playing slightly in the distance.

It was the perfect song, for the perfect moment, at the perfect time I quickly thought, and it totally took my mind off of anything else that I was thinking about.

By then, the sun had started to rise and the rain was finally easing off again. I was still over an hour away from home, but I didn't care much about that, after all, it was Sunday morning and I didn't need to be anywhere special anyway.

"I don't suppose that you'd give me a ride home now, would you?" The dark-haired woman finally said, after what seemed like an hour and a half or so of complete silence, but in reality it was only a few minutes.

"You've got to be joking, right?" I said, looking at her and wondering if she really was really brain damaged, or maybe it something else.

"I'll pay you of course, she said, as she dug into her purse pulling out a check-book, how about fifty quid?"

"Yeah right, I said, looking back at her, almost laughing at the thought of it, like I could cash that thing anyway? It would probably bounce all the way to the bank and then back again."

"No, no, it's good I promise, I've got the money in my account, she said, I just don't have credit cards anymore. Daddy ripped them all apart, just the other day in-fact. He said that I spend too much money on them."

The waitress made her way over to the table again, "Can I get you anything else Hun?" she asked, looking straight into my eyes and almost ignoring the woman like she wasn't even there.

"Just a taxi for this crazy woman here, I said smiling at her and maybe your phone number as well, which would be really nice."

The waitress, smiled back at me and said, "Sorry love, I'm a happily married woman, showing me the ring on her left hand at the same time, but thanks for asking me anyway. I'm kind of flattered that you did, because I know that someone like you could have just about any girl out there, and if I wasn't married, I'd love to go out with you sometime I'm sure, but I am married and that's that, so anyway, just let me know when you want that cab and I'll ring it through."

"No wait, the dark-haired woman said, they won't take any checks and that's all that I have, please give me a ride, she said to me again, please. I'll give you my phone number as well."

I started laughing at her for real this time. "Yeah right, I said, like I'd really want to talk to your old man, when he picks up the phone with me on the other end of the line? I'll tell you what though, you write that check out for a Grand and I'll make sure that you get home perfectly safe and sound."

"Ouch," she said, a thousand pounds? I don't think I really deserve that, but how about if I give you, say two-fifty?"

"Two hundred and fifty quid, I said, looking at her still smiling, you really are joking aren't you? And besides that, two-fifty is just taking the piss, you're gonna have to make it out for at least Five Hundred quid, and not a penny less."

"Ok, ok, she said, writing out five hundred pounds on the check, and then handing it to me. Here you go then, but you'll have to fill in your own name on the top of it; because I can't remember for the life of me, what you told me it was."

"Don't you worry about that, I said, as I took the check out of her hand? Just make sure that it doesn't bounce, because your name and address are on it as well, plain as day, and I don't want to have to come back by your house, just to collect my cash at a later date, if you know what I mean? That's not good business as far as I'm concerned, and this is strictly business now and nothing else."

"Don't worry; it's a good check, honest it is. The money's sitting in the bank already. So, no problems, no worries, she said, you'll get your money, I promise." And then, right out of the blue, like nothing else had happened between us, she said,

"Do you want to do this again next Saturday night? I could always meet you somewhere else? There's a pub around the corner from where I live actually. We could meet up there, and then maybe head out to the country after a few quick drinks of course."

I started laughing again, so hard, that I almost pissed my pants. This woman was a complete and utter lunatic I thought, who was totally off her bloody rocker.

Then I got up and went to the men's room, splashed some water on my face and looked into the mirror. I'm not a bad looking guy really, I thought, so why in the hell, did I have to put up with all of this bullshit tonight?

I dried my hands, and made my way back out to where the woman was still sitting. I sat back down for a minute or two, watching her finish what she was eating and then I started wondering what her father did to control her credit cards and what about her husband?

"So, I quickly said to her, your father tore up your credit cards huh? What's up with that then?"

"Yeah that's true, the girl said, he says that I spend way too much money on them, so he tore them all up. Why do you ask?

"Well, what about your husband, I said quickly, what does he have to say about all of that then?"

"Oh, I see what you're thinking, but it's not like that at all she said. I only got married, so that I could move away from home, while I go to school, you see?

I just live with the guy at the moment, although I suppose that's not quite how he sees it, to be honest? But you know, it's only for a little while. He's really more of a friend that I've known since I was a kid, and now we share a flat together, but Daddy pays the rent. He got mad at me for buying the food, and stuff, when my husband couldn't afford too, and I also bought a few new books for his courses as well, which he said, that he'd pay me back for, later on, when he gets a real job I suppose?

That's about all really; except that he's totally gay, my husband of course, not my Daddy, but I imagine, that I spent a little too much on the clothes though, because I always do. I love new clothes, I always have and I always will, probably even more than a little too much, really, but hey I'm a girl, and that's what girls like. Then of course, there's the pizza and beers, and the taxi cabs that we get every Friday night, and Sunday afternoon, when we go out to watch movies with our friends. But they're the ones that are already scheduled; I get a bill from them once a month."

"So you really are married then, I said, quickly interrupting her again, before she got into writing a book on the subject, but not really, is that what you're trying to tell me? And he's gay? What the fuck is that? And what was tonight all about then, and while we're at it, how old are you anyway, when you say that you're still going to school and all of that shite?"

"I'm almost twenty-one, she said, but I still have to do, whatever my father wants. He pays the bills for me. He pays my tuition and he pays the rent, what more can I say? I've got one more year of university to go and then I can do what I like.

I'll have my degree and I'll have access to my own trust account that my grandpa set-up before he died. So yeah, things will be fine, eventually.

"Let's just get out of here; I finally said to her, as I got up from the table and put my jacket back on. I'm going to need to get some sleep at some point in time and I'm hoping that that'll be sooner than later, if you know what I mean?

Trace Walton's "She's gone" was playing on the jukebox by then, which was just another great song for the moment, I thought, as I headed for the door.

I bet that guy's been through the wringer, more than just a few times himself, by the sounds of things anyway.

Then I heard the woman say. "I don't suppose that we could stop off and go skinny dipping somewhere along the way, she was grinning from ear to ear when she said it, with a look in her eyes, that anyone would have practically died for. She was so friggin beautiful it was hard to resist.

"Don't push it woman," I said back at her, smiling at the very thought of it. Maybe if I did take her down to the river, I'd get lucky and then she'd leave me alone afterwards, but I thought about that again, figuring that it wasn't such a good idea at all, still smiling though.

I paid the bill and thanked the waitress for her hospitality, by telling her to keep the change from the fifty pound note that I had just handed to her. She smiled really wide and then said, "Thank-you very much honey, you have a great day now you hear and do come back and see us again sometime." Just as the dark-haired woman, grabbed my arm in hers, having us both leave the restaurant looking as if we were an old married couple strolling out after a Sunday brunch.

She was smiling now, and still going on about swimming somewhere, but I wasn't listening to her anymore, or at least I was trying really hard not to listen. I would've liked to have laid her down just for the hell of it, but I never did married women to begin with, unless of course, I didn't know that they were married at the time that is?

Most married women make me cringe anyway; because you can never trust them especially if they're screwing around on their husbands, then you know that they'd screw around on you and everyone else as well. And besides that, they've always reminded me of those dirty old Cougar types that had fucked around with me when I was just a kid.

They were married too, but they'd just lie through their teeth about it and then kick me out of the bed right before their husband got home, if I was lucky that is? Definitely not the kind of women that I'd be associated with now that's for sure, and beside that, there's just too many, good looking, honest, single women, out there anyway, and let's face it; no-one could ever get them all, no matter how hard they tried.

Outside, the rain had finally stopped falling and the skies were starting to clear. Soon, we were off and running, out of the parking lot, down the road and completely out of sight, from those that were still sitting in the restaurant wondering what in the hell, that was all about?

It was only a matter of minutes really, until both of us were enjoying the cool, crisp, breeze, which was slowly blowing the fresh air around.

Yeah, it was a lazy Sunday morning alright, with the two of us riding on the wind, a twisted little brain-dead beauty, and a tired worn-out Biker, who would've thought?

I finally pulled up to the corner of the street where the girl lived and quickly noticed that it was an affluent up-market, high-society, type of area, with insanely large, rich and lavish, old houses, that were nestled in close amongst the trees.

Each one had a long drive to the front and then down the side of it, which was pretty nice, if you like that sort of thing?

I watched her walk up to the door, put the key in the lock, and then step inside just as quickly as she could without a seconds thought or hesitation, or even a backwards glance in my direction, as far as that goes.

In-fact, I didn't get a thank-you from her neither come to think of it, but never mind, it would be the last time that we ever crossed paths if I had my way and it wouldn't be soon enough, as far as I was concerned.

I had definitely had enough of her by then, and I just wanted some solitude, if you know what I mean? I looked down at my watch before firing up the bike again. It was a little after eight in the morning, on a clear blue sunny Sunday, with barely a cloud in the sky, or a breeze in the air.

After that, I headed home, for a much needed shower, and a long, peaceful, dreamless, kind of sleep. But the next weekend, I was scooting my way up north on my own this time, with most of my wits about me, along with a full tank of gas and an extra five hundred quid in my pocket.

There was nothing of any real importance on my mind, at that particular point in time, but there was definitely a smile on my face and it was a good ride, it always was.

✶✶✶✶✶✶✶

Postscript

When I cashed the check a few days later, I noticed that the name on it was the same last name as the first Commanding Officer that I had been assigned to, during my airborne/recon training days, in the States.

He was also English, spending twelve years in the SAS, before he did another ten years with the U.S. Special Forces. A career Colonel, who was just about as bad assed, as you could get. Well on his way to becoming a General, with all the connections that he had made during his time with her majesty's Military, and then Uncle Sam's Special Forces.

He had powerful and extremely influential friends, to say the least, some of them are still living today, but that's neither here nor there.

My point is, that he really liked me, which was good thing, because he made damn sure that I was taught the right way, right from the get-go and as quickly as I could learn, which to be honest, was exactly what I needed back then.

Anyway, I finally remembered, that I had attended a special birthday party; for the Colonel's youngest daughter, right before I was shipped off overseas the first time around. The girl was a few years younger than what I was at the time, probably about twelve or thirteen, I would imagine?

She was living at home with her folks of course, and I guess, she was going to school back then as well. We had spent some time together, talking amongst ourselves, in-between the other guests that were there about life in general really, voicing our opinions, sharing some of our hopes and dreams, as well as our desires, such as what we wanted out of life and what we hoped was in store for us in the future.

She did most of the talking and she seemed like a really nice girl, quite mature for her age and fairly intelligent with it. She came from a good family, with strong morals, great character and she had the blood of soldiers running through her veins, which of course is always something to be admired. She was also stunningly beautiful, almost perfect in every way or so it appeared to me at the time?

Once the party was over though, I had to leave her with her folks and return to base. And as life would have it, I never saw her again after that.

I also remembered that the girl had sent me a letter once or twice, over the course of my first year out, but it was so long ago now, that I couldn't really remember all that was said in it, and I never wrote back to her anyway. I don't know why really, but I guess that somehow, I just knew that it wasn't right for either one of us, or perhaps I figured that I wouldn't survive the war to begin with, who really knows?

However, I never forgot about her neither, simply because she was one of the prettiest girls that I had ever met at the time and the way that we had gotten along so well in the first place, was pretty hard for me to believe and even that much harder to forget.

The years had flown by pretty fast since then, and I had been through hell too many times to count.

I suppose that the rest of it was simply a distant memory somewhere, one that wouldn't quite fade away, stuck at the back of my young and restless mind.

We had grown into adults over time, which made it difficult for either one of us to actually recognize each other, especially after that many years apart and such a short time of being together in the first place, but regardless of that, I knew it was her back then, and that thought alone became one more thing that blew me away about that night. Who would've thought?

Its funny how life is at times, what could've, would've, should've, been? Nah, nowhere close, I thought, as I started up my motorcycle again. That was never going to be me in the first place, and I was pretty sure that it never would be.

****

With that said, I guess that's where I'm going to leave this book for now. It is only the beginning of what I'd like to write about and the stories that I want to tell you from here on out will be about others as well, simply because I get bored with my own voice more than anything, and I'm sure that there's some of you, who didn't appreciate what was written here anyway, or even liked the way I wrote it, but I thank you for coming this far, and hope that you'll stick with me as a reader to my writings.

I apologise if you didn't get anything out of this, but I haven't finished writing about the things that I want to write about, and I'm quite sure that others will have gotten something from all of this, otherwise it would be a waste of time, and I really don't want to be accused of wasting peoples time. So, Please be kind when you rate this work regardless.

They say that only 3% of those that set out to write a book in the first place will actually finish it, and less than 1% of those, will actually publish it. So I guess I'm doing alright in that department, considering everything else?

However, Sales is what fuels the fire so to speak, so please spread the word and give me five stars on Amazon, for effort if nothing else.

Anyway, be on the lookout for the next Traveller addition, sometime in the near future, and we'll meet again….cheers for now and thank-you so much for you time and support in all of this, it is very much appreciated, as always.

To be continued

T.S. DeWalt

****

Printed in Great Britain
by Amazon